Playing Time: Tough Truths about AAU Basketball, Youth Sports, Parents, and Athletes

By Kevin McNutt

Chicago, Illinois

Front cover illustration by Damon Stanford

First Edition, First Printing

Printed in the United States of America

ISBN #: 0-910030-17-0

ISBN #: 978-0-910030-17-5

CONTENTS

Dedication

To my devoted wife and two
loving daughters,
a trio truly sent from heaven.
To St. Anthony High School 1972-1974, my
teammates, classmates, friends
and teachers that made every day
spent at the little building on
Lawrence St NE a lifetime memory
of fun and education.

Introduction

In team sports, it is all about playing time. Always has been, always will be.

In the winter months of 2009, newspapers in Washington, DC, recited chapter and verse about how the city's then-mayor Adrian Fenty was using the power of his office so his nine-year-old twin sons could participate in a Department of Parks and Recreation basketball league. Apparently, the Mayor was pulling strings to have his sons compete in the eight-year-old division instead of the older one for ten-year-old players.

When a DC employee in charge of the league disputed the special request, he was allegedly fired, after which he brought a lawsuit against Fenty, the Department of Parks and Recreation Director Clark E. Ray, and the District government, alleging defamation and retaliation under DC's whistleblower protection statute.

The bottom line on the entire embarrassing story? Playing time. Fenty, like many parents in youth sports, was upset with the lack of "burn" or "bump" or "run" or "clock" that his sons were receiving. His solution, like that of so many parents with children participating in youth sports, was essentially to have his sons quit and transfer—in this case to another level of play. Except that as mayor of the nation's capital, Fenty and his solution made the newspapers.

**

This scenario has parallels even at the college level. Many of the most esteemed coaches in National Collegiate Athletic Association (NCAA) basketball are up in arms about the rising transfer rate in Division I college basketball. Tom Izzo, the head basketball coach at Michigan State, and Mike Krzyzewski of Duke University are extremely concerned and have commented about the negative impact on the game of college basketball. (Still, both have accepted transfers during the 2014 recruiting season.) Many coaches see the problem of transferring within college basketball as an "epidemic"!

Jeff Goodman, a national college basketball reporter for ESPN following the transfer issue, notes that in 2014, 522 players, or 11.4 percent of the roster players at the 351 colleges participating in Division I basketball, have transferred to another program.

To be fair, there are a multitude of reasons players leave one school and move to another. But near, if not at the top of that list of reasons is playing time, or the lack of it.

In fact, the NCAA's own research into transfers after the 2012–13 season suggests that 90 percent of transferred students in that class said they moved for "athletic reasons," which, of course, is a euphemism for wanting more playing time.

The quest for playing time has been a part of sport since the advent of team sports and the need for having a bench with substitutes. It will continue to be a key component. It is also not necessarily a bad desire for players and their parents to have. The quest for playing time can be motivating to some players as they refuse to accept their situation and become determined to work and compete harder to improve their game and change their circumstances.

Except in today's youth sports environment, with the abundance of "grass is greener" options, players and parents decide in an eye-blink to move on to other venues. In their haste to transfer, they reveal a troubling lack of patience and sense of accountability, among other things.

What's the end game here? Whether parents and players recognize it, the quest for playing time is about maximizing potential and trying to climb what I call the "Sports Pyramid," whose tip represents that much-coveted professional sports career.

***

Playing Time: Tough Truths about AAU Basketball, Youth Sports, Parents, and Athletes

Coach blew his whistle, corralled his players, and instructed us to take a seat on the cold metal bleachers that were two rows deep. It was before practice on a wintry Saturday morning at St. Anthony High School, located in the northeast section of Washington, DC. After a victory the night before, we were confused as to why practice was starting in this atypical manner instead of the customary stretching and laps around the gym floor. As far as we knew, we were not in hot water for poor performance. This morning, however, St. Anthony head basketball coach Robert Grier, as he was prone to do and as most high school coaches often do, was attempting to expand the minds of his players beyond jump shots, defensive slide drills, and preparing for our next opponent. Coach Grier was attempting to provide his players with lessons beyond the court, lessons on how basketball parallels life, lessons about preparing us to be better men and not just better basketball players.

Coach Grier proceeded to share his wisdom regarding the importance of a strong work ethic and staying committed— essentially wisdom that would guide a player up his version of that Sports Pyramid of success, which I have since personalized after decades of participating and observing youth sports. Coach, in my opinion, was conveying that being physically talented wasn't enough to reach your athletic goals and move upward. He was stressing that a combination of talent and work ethic along with personal integrity and determination would equal success. The topic was not original, but that morning, for us, the information was new. Furthermore, Coach stressed that the Sports Pyramid had relevance beyond basketball. It could be applied in any realm of life and still have value.

When viewed through that lens, Coach Grier achieved his goal: he taught his players the connection between life and sports. The conversation in 1974 only had to reach one of his players—and it definitely reached me. Coach left a lasting impression on his players beyond the wins and losses of games.

Introduction

After all, isn't that what every teacher, coach, and administrator at any institution of learning strives to do? Forty plus years later, Coach Grier's perspective on that Sports Pyramid still resides in my thoughts and those of many of my teammates.

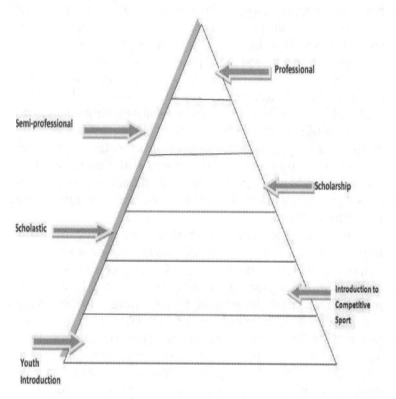

Dreamer to Professional

The concept of the Sports Pyramid is straightforward. Imagine a pyramid, a triangle. From a wide base proceed upwards to where all angles converge at the top to a sharp point.

The tip or top of the pyramid signifies the level of the professional athlete. At the expansive base, or bottom, of the pyramid is every person who has ever dreamed of playing a sport. Between the base and the apex you have tiers, or levels,

viii

of sports participation. With this illustration, it is very easy to identify the required steps to get from the sprawling base of the pyramid (youthful dreamer) to the exceptional high point (professional athlete). The path from youth to the pros is very clear—at least it was when Coach Grier pointed it out to us in the winter of 1974. The straight and paved road involved achieving athletic success at each level from high school through a four-year stay in college and then, hopefully, an opportunity to play professionally.

Since then, the sports path has blossomed into a multi-lane highway devoid of safety signs, lane markings, and speed limits, with more traffic than ever as athletes pursue upward mobility and the professional track. However, young athletes and parents uninformed about youth sports, in their zeal to advance through the steps and eventually reach the top of the pyramid, often forget a key component. They forget that in the ascent up the Sports Pyramid toward the dream career of a professional, the number of athletes reaching the top becomes smaller and smaller. The vast majority of athletes *must* fall off somewhere along the way. Young athletes and parents who are unfamiliar with the principles of the Sports Pyramid fail to realize that this is a sports law. It's not personal but predetermined by the system's design.

Principles of the Sports Pyramid

People have assigned different definitions, categories, and tiers to the Sports Pyramid. In my framework, it has six tiers: 1) Youth Introduction to Sport, 2) Youth Introduction to Organized Competitive Sport, 3) Scholastic Sport, 4) Scholarship Sport, 5) Semi-Professional, and 6) Top Professional.

Within each tier are levels and steps grouped together according to criteria such as 1) the age and skill set of the athletes (e.g., Pop Warner football), 2) the level of coaching

Introduction

and stated goals of the sports organization (state high school federation), 3) non-salary compensation (college scholarship), and 4) a contract to become an employee of a professional organization (NBA).

1. Youth Introduction to Sport. At the bottom or base is the introduction to sports and how the games are played. It is a beautiful time of innocence and imagination and spontaneity devoid of boundaries and rigidity. It is a time for children's imaginations to sprout wings. Youngsters imitate their sports heroes. Often, while at play they are making their own rules on the fly, not to gain competitive advantage as much as for the sake of convenience and fun to accommodate the numbers of players, equipment on hand, and the limitations of available space. Inclusion is the goal and fun is the prize. Every youngster starts here.

2. Youth Introduction to Organized Competitive Sport. Step up a tier on the pyramid into another area that is still spacious yet smaller than the introduction to sport. This tier includes Physical Education class, church leagues, Boys and Girls Club, Pee Wee baseball & Pop Warner football, T-ball & Little League, playground, and recreation ball. This is where youth decide if they are really interested and believe they can succeed at a given sport. Some lose interest as fun and free-flowing experimentation gives way to parental expectations, regimentation, and standards. Winning and losing leapfrog fun and imagination. Talent begins to surface as a factor in that bigger, faster, and stronger players begin to dominate and get the lion's share of attention and accolades.

3. Scholastic Sport. Move up a higher notch on the pyramid to Scholastic Sport. This involves athletic participation in middle school, junior high school, and high school sports programs with finite roster slots. Players usually must try out to make these rosters and squads. Competition intensifies and talent and potential become important factors. It is at this tier where issues start to become murky, where lines are crossed, agendas and alliances formed. In today's billion-dollar youth sports field, the battle for scholarships and the pursuit for playing time becomes paramount. Parents and adults become more vested and involved. Conventional boundaries, such as neighborhoods, age limits, and grade standards, become blurred, compromised, redrawn, disregarded, or omitted, as money, ego, and the backroom agendas of adults take root in order to establish either the best environment for young athletes to excel or acquire the best players for teams to win.

Athletic recruiting intensifies, loyalty is discouraged, and accountability is plea-bargained. Competitive club and travel programs have strongly infiltrated this particular area and age group (13–17), but due to serious competition, for most athletes these outlets generally offer more athletic memories than next-level athletic scholarships and opportunities to advance.

Meanwhile, the pyramid continues to narrow. In fact, this tier on the athletic pyramid is where the majority of athletic careers and sports dreams dissolve. It is also the most painful as many parents and athletes realize that the athletic scholarship to college is not forthcoming. It hits hard like an angry tide rushing over its banks during a tropical storm. After the all-or-nothing pursuit of an athletic scholarship proves fruitless, the recognition presents a financial hardship for many parents to get their athlete to college at all, much less to play a sport there. Meanwhile, for the high-school athlete, coming to grips with the end of the adulation, campus-star status, and prospect for a college athletic career is a tough jolt to the ego. The new reality—recreation and church leagues on a weeknight or a weekend—is a serious kick in the stomach.

4. Scholarship Sport. For those fortunate and talented enough to continue their athletic career beyond high school, the next level on the pyramid is college. This includes all the various NCAA divisions—I, II, and III—the National Association of Intercollegiate Athletics (NAIA), and the National Junior College Athletic Association (NJCAA). The key denominator in reaching this level on the pyramid is talent, and talent that is recognized. Players are offered scholarships and financial aid packages for their athletic gifts and their potential to help colleges reach goals for their sports programs. While not an exact science, athletes are recruited, scouted, judged, and analyzed for a select few roster spots. On occasion mistakes are made in assessing athletic talent and a small percentage of athletes attend college without a scholarship (they are considered "walk-ons").

It should be noted that many athletes and parents do not realize just how fortunate players are to be able to continue their careers past high school, especially with financial assistance or an athletic scholarship. For example, a college of 20,000 students that participates in 20 NCAA sports, has roughly 400–500 athletes on campus, or less than 1 percent of the student body playing collegiate sports.

Yet, most college athletes and specifically those who start for their football or basketball teams, regardless of their school's NCAA division classification, believe that with the "right breaks" they will play professionally. Meanwhile, the athletic pyramid continues to narrow.

5. Semi-Professional. Still further up the pyramid is the Semi-Professional level. This entails the minor leagues in baseball or the D-League (Developmental League) in the NBA. Talented athletes enter into contracts for their services. Here, the pyramid is near its highest point.

6. Top Professional. Finally, at the top of the pyramid is the elite professional. These are the most gifted athletes in the world. They are also some of the most dedicated, hardest-working, tough and single-minded, committed, competitive and passionate people you will ever meet. In the NBA, for example, these athletes hold one of the most coveted fifteen team roster spots in all of sports.

The entire Sports Pyramid is about high supply and low demand. The higher an athlete climbs on the athletic pyramid, the smaller the number of roster spots, thus ensuring an inevitable and obvious fall for most of those seeking the top of the pyramid. Consider that each season over a half million athletes play high school basketball, but only 450 play in the NBA.

Ascending and Descending the Pyramid
The number one reason players ascend the Sports Pyramid is plain and simple: they have athletic talent. Certain athletes, even as young teens, project professional stardom. NBA stars LeBron James and Kevin Durant, the NFL's Andrew Luck and Calvin "Megatron" Johnson, and Major League Baseball's Stephen Strasburg and Mike Trout come to mind. And yet, even the talent of these gifted athletes needed allies. Talent needs commitment and passion and work ethic. Talent needs opportunity, luck, exposure, timing, nurturing, dedication, and coaching. Regardless of the tier on which athletes are performing on the Sports Pyramid, any and all athletes must have all these attributes and resources.

It is within the more overlooked tiers of the Sports Pyramid, specifically Scholastic to Scholarship, that more young athletes are having a premature fall from the Sports Pyramid. This is a serious concern and deserves intense scrutiny. As the following chapters will demonstrate, for many young basketball players that premature fall stems from a multitude of youth sports scenarios from the questionable practices of certain AAU, club and travel programs to the misguided decisions of parents who, unbeknownst to them, hinder the athletic development of their children. What I've learned and what I share here about the development of young players—the good *and* the bad—has been informed by observations over forty-plus years—as a scholastic and collegiate player, an AAU and high school coach, referee, and dedicated parent of a scholarship basketball player.

Talent, commitment and passion, making good life-changing decisions away from the sport, and an excellent work ethic are all easy and identifiable factors guiding an athlete's ascent up the Pyramid. However, there is another pressing factor: the role of parents.

In today's intense youth sports climate, with the multitude of choices and options available to families and young athletes, parents' decisions regarding playing time and the development of their athlete through the different stages are more critical than ever. Never before have the decisions of the parent been so numerous and so instrumental in the growth of their athlete at such a young age. The decisions of parents won't necessarily hinder or suppress the supreme talents of the prodigy; however, they are more impactful in determining if their child plays high school athletics at all or will start on his/her high school team or has an opportunity to play college sports on scholarship at any level.

In the forty years since my introduction to the Sports Pyramid, the scope of parental involvement and decision-making has taken on an entirely different dynamic. Sure, parents have and will always be a huge part of the upbringing of their child athletes. They should be. However, the intensity, drive, unbridled passion and aggression, egotism, obsession with living vicariously, cunning, mercenary thinking, vitriol, naïveté, shortsightedness, erroneous perceptions, and general lack of sports knowledge of those uninitiated to youth sports today is alarming and disheartening.

And it is not entirely their fault.

Youth sports have become a multi-billion dollar industry. Parents are bombarded in every venue of sports, at every age of their child's participation in sports from two to twenty-two by advertisers offering assistance and remedies, or hawking shortcuts to help them reach their athletic dreams.

The mindboggling list of choices and options for parents is seemingly endless and includes the following:

1. Off-Season Games and Tournaments. This arena consists of the notorious and usual suspects such as club teams, travel teams, Pop Warner football, and AAU basketball that offer a dizzying assortment of games and more games. They want your membership dues and fees. They want your monies for your child to compete in their out-of-town tournaments even for players as young as eight years old. (A national tournament for nine-year-olds is preposterous. It is a farcical event that means nothing to the child who can't tell a single difference between tournament hosting cities such as Richmond, Virginia, versus Dayton, Ohio, or stay accommodations such as Red Roof versus Holiday Inn Express. It is nothing more than a dream-selling, money-grabbing, ego-tripping, keeping-up-with-the-Joneses sham intended for the uninformed parent with a credit card.)

2. Private School Athletic Programs. They need your tuition payments to help offset declining enrollments. They see the financial benefits, along with an increase in popularity and visibility in the community and with alumni, when they have outstanding athletic teams. Consequently, recruiting athletic talent serves as an important source of fundraising revenue. However, their recruiting is broad and inclusive, which means the number of athletes and parents they sell dreams to far exceed the number of roster spots available on the teams. It is thus a creation of their version of the Sports Pyramid.

3. Summer Camps. The once benign and wholesome adventure of attending summer sports camps has become a very competitive and expensive enterprise. For uninformed parents, trying to find a summer camp that is affordable yet fits their athlete's interest, skill level, age group, and competitive level can be a daunting task. Parents sometimes feel they need a guidance counselor just to help with the selection process. In many instances, camps have become so specialized that they have morphed from all-inclusive, generic entities such as basketball camps or baseball camps to fancy-title specialty clinics appealing to a specific position such as quarterback, pitcher, big man, or point guard. These skills camps focus on the teachings, fundamentals, details, and nuances of mastering a position. This, of course, appeals to the parent who believes that the specialized teaching gives their athletic child an insight and advantage over the competition.

4. Personal Trainers. Then there is the unregulated sect of personal trainers offering individual and/or group rates—with an emphasis on groups to financially maximize each ninety-minute session. This is a rapidly expanding army of former collegiate or pro players with flashy business cards and sports-achievement websites. Most do have a base of expertise that can help aspiring athletes. However, *knowing* something and *teaching* something are two different things, and many trainers conduct business in a haphazard manner due primarily to the lack of access to facilities conducive to maximum learning.

5. Sports Psychiatrists. These doctors, a new addition to the equation, work with young athletes to help them through their problems and inhibitions as they relate to sports achievement. Parents with deep enough pockets to pay $200 an hour are sending their young athletes from ages ten and up to work through their various in-game competition anxieties.

6. Quick-Fix Salesmen and Their Inventions. These are the medicine, vitamin, supplement, magic-potion, and elixir salesmen, accompanied by state-of-the-art-technology and equipment/gear gurus and companies offering pie-in-the-sky testimonials. Their products will supposedly improve everything from an athlete's jumping/vertical leap to his or her height (that's right, increasing *height*), strength, weight, vision, forty-yard speed time, hand-eye coordination, endurance, stamina, and quick thinking/mental concentration, all to give your child an edge in getting to the next level and becoming a star.

7. New Age Inventions. Even Nike, the kingpin of youth sports sneakers and gear, can't resist the temptation to capitalize on the easy sell of athletic dreams. In November 2011, Nike introduced its SPARQ Vapor Strobe eyewear. These eyeglasses, retailing at $300, featured a strobe-lighting effect that allegedly developed quicker reaction times and motor skills. (I know of several single moms, under tight budgets but seeking every advantage, who paid out in pursuit of a scholarship for their athlete.) Eighteen months later, Nike chose to discontinue the item for unannounced reasons. Not surprisingly, the Amateur Athletic Union (AAU) couldn't resist acting on its greed by way of easy victims desperate to buy anything to fulfill their athletic dreams. So the organization produced a slick, ego-gratifying annual directory of the "best" AAU players in the country. The 2013 edition contained statistical bios of 5,000 players, some as young as eight years old. While being the "best" is undefined, apparently just having your athlete's name next to past greats of the AAU, like Lebron James, makes the $60 price tag of the directory inconsequential.

8. Movie Directors. Let's not forget the Madison Avenue-type advertisers and sports dream sellers who will market your athlete's newfound athletic gifts and get his or her glossy video package to the right people, like college coaches and recruiters. These folks will produce and edit your stellar practice workouts and game tapes, enhance your résumé and profile, and forward it to the 150 schools that need to know about your athlete's under-the-radar talent; hopefully a scholarship offer will follow. The cost for the package can range from $100 to north of $900.

The Secret

Most of these endeavors and services potentially can be beneficial to the sports skill development and enhancement of your child and to the fulfillment of their athletic goals. Most are comprised of professional people who are very capable and committed to their enterprise.

Yet this is an ever-growing fraternity that, through the aid of social media, has gained easy access to the uninformed parent in search of any advantage to get playing time for their child. The options and choices, today more than ever before, are bewildering and, of course, costly. As in all transactions, buyers beware.

The one thing that is missing with all of these entities is accountability, which these sports dream-selling businesses will not offer you. Why? Because they already know what uninformed parents need to know: 1) there are no guarantees to achieving Sports Pyramid next-level success (generally, getting an athletic scholarship or even increasing playing time), and 2) success is ultimately dependent on the work ethic, determination, commitment, and passion of the athlete. There are no shortcuts or quick fixes, no substitutes for hard work, practice, and repetition. All of these money-making enterprises understand this, but as profit-making entities, they flood the market with opportunities to sell athletic dreams without accountability.

The Effect
These promises that are constantly in parents' faces short circuit them and heighten their frustration and anxiety, especially when they pay substantially for only minimal results. However, the process of trying to make their child athlete better need not be such an urgent, sports life-or-death endeavor. Wanting to assist and support their child is a good thing. Decisions to purchase certain products and services can be a good thing. It becomes a problem when parents believe these solutions to be the end game or the automatic quick fix.

The quick-fix approach is a colossal mistake and the prime example of how parents' decisions can lead to their athlete falling from the Sports Pyramid. Nothing replaces hard work, practice, and repetition—not participating on a soccer travel team or sending a tape to a college. In fact, in most cases, quick fixes will reveal the lack of those essentials.

The Blame Game
There are other, more subtle decisions parents make that may send their athletic children toward an early fall from the

pyramid. Many parents do not hold their children or themselves accountable during the athletic journey. Parents, frequently make multi-faceted excuses for not realizing certain athletic goals. Of course, it's so often someone else's fault. But the bottom line is, when athletes are not held accountable, excuse making and the blame game take hold. The fault doesn't lie solely with these athletes. How can they be held accountable when the parents themselves haven't first looked in the mirror at their own deportment?

Often, poor parental behavior starts early—for example, simple irresponsible conduct at games, especially at preteen sports contests. Overly intense parents primarily and frequently badger and berate referees. They boldly dispense criticism to opposing fans, teams, and players, and even on occasion to the home team coaches. These are horrible examples of sportsmanship and only set the table for creating alibis, as children are intently watching this boorish behavior. Predictably, on the way home, those same parents will blame the "blind" and "sorry" referees, the absent-minded coach, the deplorable visitor facilities—everybody or everything but their own hot-headed temper and foul mouths.

It is amazing that parents cannot connect the dots to see that impressionable athletes who want to please their parents will eventually, in some manner, incorporate this behavior and excuse-making into their own demeanor on the court/ field. At the very least, young athletes are noticing the erosion of respect for authority, and they feel encouraged to challenge or question command. This makes athletes torn in their allegiances and, in some cases, confrontational. It is a slippery slope that can lead to a potentially early fall from the Sports Pyramid.

Almost immediately in an athlete's career, a peripatetic journey of transferring schools ensues with the parents in butterfly mode, flitting from place to place for the right situation that will allow their athlete to shine above others. Transferring has its place and is necessary on occasion. However, transferring to four or more different schools in a four-year high school career is usually a major red flag that has "lack of accountability" written all over it. Having that many athletic homes sends the false message to players that they are blameless, that the situation and program is wrong, and that they are not accountable but merely the victim. (This scenario is historically more prevalent in boys' high school sports, but in recent years girls, with equal college scholarship chances, seem to be transferring just as frequently.)

Decisions to transfer have repercussions at the higher levels of sport. Accountability as well as trust is lost, and college coaches may have reservations in considering the athlete for a scholarship. Generally these coaches' instincts are right. Once the transfer-obsessed, nomadic lifestyle starts, it often repeats itself as the parent and athlete never find the elusive, perfect, happy sports home.

The issue here is ultimately about loyalty. If parents acting on a whim continuously move their athlete from travel team to travel team, from high school to high school, loyalty has clearly taken a back seat. Because good coaches plan for programs, not just individual seasons, they want athletes they can trust and count on, not takers and "me-first" artists.

In special cases, talent will trump all, but when two equally talented athletes collide for a championship title or perhaps the last available scholarship, intangibles such as conviction, purpose, fortitude, and character will determine who moves forward. If an athlete has a track record of lacking accountability and of placing blame elsewhere, he or she will not compete when it matters most.

Parents can be so impulsive, overbearing, and demanding regarding playing time and upward movement on the Sports

Pyramid that the athlete gets caught in the crossfire. In certain instances a coach will simply grow weary and suggest the athlete and family move on. At that point, parents have been deemed total hands-on micro-managers. They have become more trouble to deal with than having the player in the program. This scenario, almost unheard of decades ago when our culture was less sports-obsessed, is more commonplace now as the pressures continually increase for parents to ensure their athletes excel and move up the Sports Pyramid.

Chapter 1: The Youth Sports Launching Pad: The Big Three (Plus One)

In the 1980s and early 1990s, three game-changing developments converged on all sports, and specifically inner-city youth basketball, in urban cities such as Washington, DC, and erupted like lava from a volcano. These ruptures, which I call "the Big Three," shook and reshaped not only youth basketball but all of youth sports and the dreams and aspirations of sports parents.

These developments were the launch of Michael Jordan's advertising relationship with Nike, the growth of ESPN, and the rise of Tiger Woods. All three developments helped initiate the astronomical growth of the dream-selling business in youth sports, the transformation of youth sports especially as it relates to parents' goal-setting for their children, and the long-established presence of AAU and competitive travel basketball in the black community.

This triumvirate of change, all taking place within a similar timespan, facilitated the stampede that today is manifested in several ways:

1. A multi-billion-dollar youth sports industry

2. The frenetic rush to promote young people to sports prominence while stripping them of their youth

3. The selfish me-first, gotta-get-mine, by-any-means-necessary determination and desperation of parents

4. The confusion of uninformed parents lost in a dizzying maze of youth sports products, services, and promises,

desperately selling out to pursue that athletic scholarship for their child to which they incorrectly believe he or she is entitled.

5. The erosion and surrender of time-tested values and principles (e.g., hard work, patience, fundamentals, sacrifice, commitment) that were prevalent before the convergence of the Big Three and, although still accessible, have largely been replaced by ego, greed, impatience, selfishness, and a lack of accountability and sports knowledge.

Michael and Nike

Michael Jordan entered the 1984 NBA draft after a stellar three-year basketball career at the University of North Carolina. There he was mentored by legendary Hall of Fame coach Dean Smith, and he helped his team win the 1982 NCAA basketball championship by nailing the game deciding fifteen-foot jumper with seconds remaining. He would become the third player taken in that draft by the Chicago Bulls. One of the greatest basketball players of all time, Jordan enjoyed a Hall of Fame career that included winning six NBA championships with the Bulls.

Jordan also proved to be a Hall of Fame advertising phenomenon. In 1984, he signed a shoe contract with Nike. At the time it was a dicey, high-stakes, high-priced proposal for even Phil Knight, the risk-taking founder of Nike. The contract exceeded the going rate that other athletic shoe companies like Converse and Adidas paid to already established NBA stars.

The risk paid off. Knight and Nike had won the lottery as everything came up roses. Jordan became an instant star. With his high flying dunking show, one-on-one captivating moves, live, active, and energetic body, and effervescent personality and smile, he would score over twenty-eight points per game and receive the NBA Rookie of the Year award. A generation of kids wanted to "Be Like Mike," quoting a TV commercial featuring Jordan.

Taking flight just as fast as the Chicago Bull All Star were his Air Jordan sneakers. Commissioner David Stern unintentionally gave Nike a free advertisement when, in October '84, he banned the shoe for not complying with league color standards. Sales instantly took off, and requests for the sneakers exceeded even Nike's goals. Only two months after the sneaker made its debut in March 1985, Nike had sold $70 million worth. By year's end, the Air Jordan franchise had yielded more than $100 million in revenues.

In the company's annual report that year, Knight called it "the perfect combination of quality product, marketing and athlete endorsement."

The Jordan-Nike relationship was in high gear now, blowing the competition clean away. In 1984, Nike's total revenue was about $900 million. By 1997, when Jordan was closing in on the fifth of his six NBA titles, revenue hit $9.19 billion.

Beginning in the 1980s, the entire youth sports industry took notice and the pursuit to get its share naturally became priority number one. Michael Jordan and Nike changed the model of how businesses market to youth. With millions of dollars available to the industry, established traditions, protocols, and procedures were nearly obliterated. The sneaker war was on, and youth sports and dreams would become the battlefield.

Chapter 1: The Youth Sports Launching Pad: The Big Three (Plus One)

ESPN

The Entertainment and Sports Programming Network (ESPN) made its debut on September 7, 1979, and clearly, sports programming and television watching were forever changed. Bill Rasmussen and his son, Scott Rasmussen, founded the twenty-four-hour network, and experts thought the concept had no chance to survive. At the time there were no twenty-four-hour networks—not ABC, CBS, NBC, or even HBO. The Fox network, CNN, and MTV hadn't been thought of yet.

Yet here came ESPN with a vision to set the television industry on its heels. Starting with only one location in Bristol, Connecticut—one 10,000 square-foot building on one acre of land, one domestic network, 1.3 million subscribers, and 80 employees—ESPN is now the gold standard for sports television. Its four-letter moniker is perhaps the most famous combination of letters ever. Today ESPN, the Worldwide Leader in Sports, reaches more than 100 million US households and undoubtedly is watched at some point during the day by anybody and everybody that calls himself or herself a sports fan. Many sports folk call *SportsCenter*, the station's news and highlights show, the most important and best program on all of television.

In the early 1980s, ESPN was still looking for its niche. The network carried a lot of ancillary sports just to fill in time slots. But soon basketball, specifically NCAA basketball, came to the rescue. The network and the NCAA formed an alliance to show its games. In the middle-to-late 1980s, you could easily say that ESPN was the network for regular season NCAA basketball. The NCAA tournament was carried by NBC, then CBS.

4

What gave the ESPN network its NCAA credibility was the contract it signed with an up-and-coming, newly created conference named the Big East. The conference, which contained schools in large urban cities, featured Washington, DC's Georgetown University, New York City's St. John's University, its upstate neighbor Syracuse University, New Jersey rival Seton Hall University, Philadelphia's Villanova University, Boston College, its neighbor University of Connecticut, University of Pittsburgh, and Providence College. This conference would become the best college basketball conference in the country, an honor cemented when three of its teams (Georgetown, Villanova, and St. John's) went to the 1984 Final Four, a feat that until that time had never been done and has never been duplicated since.

Young viewers in large numbers tuned in to the Big East games. So powerful and impressionable to youth was the union between the Big East conference and ESPN that Jim Boeheim, the Hall of Fame coach of Syracuse who had the second most wins by a coach in NCAA history, paid tribute to the network for helping recruit athletes from the West Coast to his program. Boeheim accurately noted how West Coast athletes would be coming home from school in the late afternoon to watch the Big East games that were just starting on the East Coast, thus exposing them to Syracuse and other East Coast teams and making it easier for him and his staff to sell his program to young athletes.

ESPN changed what sports fans watched on television and in the process altered, if not revolutionized, the thought process of parents and their athletic children.

5

Chapter 1: The Youth Sports Launching Pad: The Big Three (Plus One)

Tiger Woods

Nearly every sports fan has repeatedly seen the YouTube clip of then two-year-old Eldrick "Tiger" Woods hitting a golf ball on *The Mike Douglas Show* in 1978. It was our first introduction to Tiger, who would go forward in golf to become the number one player and one of most recognized sports figures in the world. Tiger, under the tutelage and watchful eye of his father Earl, became the embodiment of a youth sports prodigy committed exclusively to one sport at a very young age (in Tiger's case two years old).

Prior to his historic win by twelve strokes in the 1997 Masters Tournament in Augusta, Georgia, at twenty-one years old, which made him the youngest golfer to ever win the event, Tiger was a young golf genius. Word of his accomplishments and golfing feats at the ages of three and five years of age landed him and Earl in golf publications and on television shows. At eight years old, Tiger won the 9-10 Division of the Junior World Championships. As an amateur he won twenty-one events, including six Junior World Championships, compiling one of the greatest amateur careers ever.

Even before Tiger became a professional, everyone wanted to know about the relationship between Tiger and his father and how he could be such a sports phenomenon. Another point of interest was the fact that this son of a black man and Asian mother was defeating older, white men at the historically exclusive game of golf. Not just golfing enthusiasts, but general sports fans, other ethnic groups, and even sports parents were interested in the mysterious development of Tiger Woods.

When Woods turned professional, he repeated the success of his amateur career, dominating the PGA tour, often besting white men twice his age in a sport all but devoid of color. His aura continued to grow. Woods has won seventy-nine times on the PGA tour, including fourteen Majors—the Masters (four times), the US Open (three), the British Open (three), and the PGA Championship (four). He has won the second most Majors in golf history, trailing only Jack Nicholas with eighteen.

During his adolescent and amateur career in the late '80s and '90s, Tiger Woods set a very high bar while establishing a framework for what can be accomplished by a young athlete at a very young age. Parents watched diligently, noting the details of the relationship between the young Tiger and his father Earl and the athletic success that ensued.

The Impact

Michael Jordan and Nike set the bar for the volume of big money that a professional athlete can make through product endorsements. In the wake of his success, an emerging industry began selling sports dreams directly to parents and indirectly to youth. And as a result a full-scale pedal-to-the-metal, dash-for-the-cash race ensued once businesses noticed in awe just how much money was to be made not only from sneakers but youth sports in general. Jordan and Nike's successful relationship fostered a let's-get-rich corporate mission that was reminiscent of the 1890s gold rush—only in this one the gold diggers wore suits.

ESPN illustrated how big people's appetite was to watch sports around the clock. They wanted not just sport events but sports talk, sports highlights, sports of all kinds, pre-game and post-game analysis. ESPN mesmerized sports fans' thinking and changed their viewing habits. The network filled the airwaves with more live sports and showed, as with Jordan and Nike, just how much money was to be had through round-the-clock sports programming. Meanwhile, because the world of sport became easier to connect with, the dreams of parents and young athletes blossomed. Tangible examples of the fulfillment of those dreams were on display all day, every day.

The Tiger Woods story gave direction, knowledge, and confidence to parents on how to take their child from self-proclaimed sports youth prodigy to the next once-in-a-generation sports icon. Parents and young athletes alike realized the need to start very early, develop determination and single-mindedness (through commitment to one sport and one sport only), and dream about achieving sports-idol status and the high-living pot o' gold promised at the end of the athletic rainbow.

The impact of the triumvirate of events covered all the bases for youth sports today. It provided a rocket-launch assist to parents in reaching their athletic dreams for their children. The Jordan and Nike relationship supplied corporate money, interest, commitment, and top quality gear and product. ESPN presented exposure, a daily witness of sports accomplishments, hope visualized, and a precedent that athletic dreams can, indeed, flourish and become reality. It was a day-to-day picture of how obsessed we are with sports and the high-pedestal, grandiose lifestyles of our sports heroes. The Tiger Woods story delivered the greatest living example of the path a child sports prodigy takes to become the most illustrious and celebrated athlete of all time. This blueprint showed parents how to create a sports superstar through a hands-on, micro-managed, committed, focused, visionary, and determined effort.

The Tiger Woods story, in particular, shows the dramatic convergence of the Big Three and the way the developments built off one another. ESPN captured Tiger's ascent on camera and cable television with an unprecedented up-close-and-personal daily televised stream, captivating the imaginations of parents and their children, giving flight to their dreams. The Michael Jordan-Nike relationship provided the corporate support and money and product backing to keep Tiger preeminent. The Big Three convergence at essentially the same time sent the aspirations and dreams of parents and young athletes soaring, while sending the entire sports world spinning to a happy and unforeseen state of sports euphoria and entertainment.

The Storm Cloud

Michael Jordan and Nike are still the most profitable sports advertising marriage ever as the twenty-ninth Jordan sneaker was just released in April 2014.

ESPN is the unquestioned gold standard in sports programming. Often imitated but never duplicated, ESPN has legendary clout and supreme control over sports viewing and programming.

The Tiger Woods story continues. He finished the 2013 season as PGA Player of the Year.

Yet regarding youth sports, the convergence of the Big 3 from twenty-five years ago has left many a casualty over the same period. Today, youth sports are out of control on so many levels. While the Big Three spawned the sports dreams of many parents and their athletic children, multitudes have found only sports nightmares.

The Big Three intensified our push for youth athletic success. It made kings and queens of our youth before they understood the throne and the responsibilities they would have to bear. Meanwhile, parents oftentimes resembled nothing more than court jesters as their emotions and egos and desperation amounted to buffoonery. Family structures were turned upside down as sports prodigies become the central figure, the future "meal ticket," as families chased athletic dreams with their foundation in quicksand.

ESPN played its part in the youth sports craze. For example, needing to fill time slots on its networks, ESPN once televised Pop Warner football playoffs featuring preteens in their trumped-up championships. Soon, high school basketball all star games, such as the McDonald's All American Game, were televised nationally. Then, realizing the low production cost to produce the games and the high fan interest and profit margin, the network started televising made-for-TV contests featuring the best teams from different areas in match-ups in both high school basketball and football.

The Tiger Woods story had parents and their athletic youth buying a one-way athletic train ticket to sports stardom and accomplishment. Parents mimicked the Tiger blueprint. They had their athlete commit to playing one sport exclusively at age three, as Tiger did. Clearly, their selection of a given sport was at the parent's discretion. How can youngsters decide which sport they want to devote all their energy and time to if they haven't played any? Thus, opportunities for youth to achieve and possibly star in other sports never materialized as playing these sports was deemed a waste of time or distraction. After all, parents thought, Tiger never seriously played another sport such as baseball, football, or soccer.

Parents began enlisting, at significant cost, the services of sports specialists and trainers to assist with individualized instruction. While it was a good idea to solicit help relating to a game's nuances and fundamentals, parents failed to answer two critical questions in embracing the Tiger Woods story: 1) Did their prodigy truly have next-level talent (a very hard assessment for sports parents to make objectively)? 2) Did their athlete have true passion for the sport, the type of passion and drive that would keep him committed and on pace despite any and all obstacles, defeats, and setbacks? Once again, another very difficult question to answer objectively when it is uncertain if the athlete is playing for the parent or him/herself.

However, the most significant difference between the Tiger Woods story and the dream it inspired for parents, and what parents seemingly failed to understand, is that golf is an individual sport and not a team one. Basketball, football, soccer, volleyball, and others are teamwork-dependent sports; golf is not.

Perhaps parents lack loyalty to any one athletic program because their detailed plan of athletic success for their prodigy has been based on the Tiger Woods model; the problem is that the model is for solo sport, not team sports. Woods was playing against the golf course, against himself. He did not, for the most part, require support from teammates. Parents have used an individual sports blueprint to develop their athlete in a team sport. As a result, they discounted the

11

Chapter 1: The Youth Sports Launching Pad: The Big Three (Plus One)

importance of dealing with coaches and teammates to reach their goal.

You can't succeed in team sports, such as basketball and football, without teammates. Yet parents can't control teammates and coaches, and if they feel those individuals are blocking the advancement of their prodigy, patience runs thin. In those cases, the carefully crafted blueprint for athletic success runs into potential jeopardy because of the perceived inadequacies of the teammates and coaches. So the parents decide that the grass is greener at another location. The "transfer train" is underway—all in pursuit of playing time and athletic prominence, per the example of the Tiger Woods story.

The Man with A Plan

While ESPN and the Tiger Woods story had an unintentional negative impact on many sports families, what transpired from the Jordan-Nike relationship was calculated and premeditated.

As soon as the athletic shoe companies found financial success and realized the power of the Jordan-Nike relationship, their quest was to find the next Jordan, the next NBA star who could sell millions of sneakers by playing nightly on this new cable network called ESPN. Since the 1970s, Nike was paying college coaches to outfit their teams in their specific sneaker.

However this arrangement wasn't good enough as the athletic shoe company decided that they needed to latch onto high school stars. Their rational was twofold: if they could establish a brand loyalty with a high school player, it would be the easier to convince him to go to a college where players already wore their sneaker. Also, if the college team continued to be strong, having recruited the best player(s), that would lead to more televised games and deep runs into the NCAA tournaments. That outcome would in turn lead to more youngsters seeing the companies' sneakers, and then buying them.

The principal corporate goal always remained intact: to find the next Jordan faster than their competition.

The challenge that arose was how to find the next superstar, the next Jordan at the high school level (or below), without essentially outfitting every team in the country. What was the most cost effective way to introduce a company's sneaker to young athletes, specifically basketball players, establish brand loyalty, and at the same time evaluate and assess the athletic potential of these hoop prodigies to not only become collegiate stars but NBA superstars? What was the best way to reach this market, and who was the best person to evaluate athletic potential?

That man proved to be John Paul "Sonny" Vaccaro. Labeled by some an entrepreneur, a pioneer, a visionary, a street hustler, or worse, Vaccaro is commonly known as "the godfather of summer basketball." No matter how he was addressed, for over thirty years Vaccaro was the most dominant, controversial, and influential man in the industry. He was to scholastic and scholarship basketball and sneakers what Muhammad Ali was to boxing.

Vaccaro was the first to pay college coaches to outfit their teams in Nike shoes. His work led to college athletic programs becoming synonymous with specific brands, such as Nike or Adidas or Reebok. As founder of the original All-Star high school basketball game, clearly Vaccaro was an out-of-the-box, innovative thinker.

When Vaccaro began landing sneaker deals with colleges, he was already on the payroll of Nike. He also already ran one of the best high school basketball post-season all-star games, the Roundball Classic. This was America's original high school All-Star Classic, which began as the Dapper Dan Roundball Classic in Pittsburgh forty-three years ago. The most widely imitated event in prep basketball, this charitable classic annually brought together the twenty-two most gifted high school all stars in the country, and holds the all-time attendance record for a high school all star event.

Vaccaro was also the cofounder of the prestigious ABCD basketball camp, established in 1984. Over the years, it had become the standard-bearer of summer camps, as the best players in high school basketball from around the country would end the unofficial spring and summer basketball season with a late-July visit to New Jersey for the five-day hoops festival.

Basketball camps and all-star games were seemingly sprouting up overnight. Vaccaro, always a step ahead of the competition, became one of the first promoters to have Nike funnel money into the spring and summer youth basketball scene.

It seemed such an easy and natural progression. The popularity of camps and all star games was growing because it brought together the best players and enhanced city rivalries while producing exciting and intriguing basketball. Yet the all star games and camps were brief spring flings lasting only a weekend or one week, leaving plenty of summer time for more basketball. Also, only a finite number of players could participate. The games and the camps barely touched the surface of talented athletes playing basketball.

So what better way to get more athletes involved than to sponsor summer teams? What better way to establish brand loyalty and corner the market of a burgeoning group of young athletes, promote the game of basketball, provide an opportunity for athletes to get better while playing better competition, have the best athletes from various neighboring high schools come together in the name of city pride, and highlight the upcoming and future stars of the game? As an added bonus, Nike could get the goodwill publicity of helping fledging city youth services. They could also assist young people, especially the black athletes so attracted and attached to basketball, get exposure and opportunities to athletic scholarships and higher education.

Oh, what a plan. It was airtight and unassailable. Surely, in the black community, once again corporate America's laboratory for product testing, expanding opportunities to play more basketball in the spring and summer at supposedly no financial cost to the black athletes could have no downside. After all, you were just coming to their neighborhoods, as protector, guardian and overseer to rescue them. It was an easy connect-the-dots scenario. They were going to play basketball anyway.

Indeed, the philosophy and plan were ingenious and paralleled the Big 3 arrival on the youth scene during the same era, the middle and late 1980s. Especially as observed in Washington, DC, competitive spring and summer ball and the AAU took meteoric flight with increasing levels of youth participation. It was the latest shiny new sports car introduced into the neighborhood. Every young athlete wanted a ride, and every adult wanted a turn at the wheel to take this fancy car for a spin around the sports block.

What could possibly be wrong with this picture, this new and innovative marketing concept and business model?

How about almost everything? And specifically in the black sports community. In fact, within these spring and summer basketball leagues, so many positives have given way to far more negatives that Vaccaro, now retired from youth sports, has in contemplation arrived at a totally different view of his original invention. Some thirty years later, he now calls spring and summer basketball a "cesspool."

Chapter 2: The Tricky Relationship between AAU Basketball and the Black Sports Community

In the 1980s, major athletic shoe companies infused new money into the urban youth sports basketball community at a time when city budgets were stretched and funding for youth services, especially recreation, were on the chopping block. Supporting AAU basketball and travel basketball in general seemed like a good idea and a win-win proposition for both the athletic shoe companies and black youth.

Indeed, it would seem like a great idea from the standpoint of corporate marketing executives who only had a cursory knowledge of the black urban community but had a primary goal to make money. Moreover, what you really had was, once again, corporate suits looking down from their pristine, ivory towers and using black youth as the test balloon for their money-making ideas. Furthermore, this larceny within the black community was taking place under the slipshod and tricky moniker of "grassroots basketball," suggesting purely humanitarian motives.

Clearly, when you determine the game, have the most money, set up the rules, bulldoze over any and all opposition, change and shift gears at any time to meet your needs, what you have established is far closer to a monopoly than an altruistic mission-driven organization. Thus, to imply on any level that the athletic shoe companies' intentions were grassroots-based or philanthropic is disingenuous, deceitful, and in the language of the city streets, a "hustle" move.

Had the athletic shoe companies taken the proper time to conduct their due diligence and research beyond the dollar potential of the black community, if they had gone beyond the shallow assessment that the "best basketball equals the best inner-city black youth," they could have seen the other side of things and damage they could inflict. Then again, that mentality is not aligned with the corporate mission. Athletic shoe companies are profits driven, and to that end, the investment into grassroots basketball was and is hugely successful.

So armed with the lessons derived from the Big 3—there is big money to be made through youth sports (Michael Jordan and Nike); there is more big money to be made through ESPN's 24/7 sports coverage and its viewers (young athletes and their parents); and the path to a sports career begins at birth (the Tiger Woods story)—the sneaker companies implemented their marketing plan of sponsoring youth basketball teams in the spring and summer through the usual petri-dish target: the black community.

The athletic shoe companies did not know that youth, basketball, and money would make for a combustible mix in the inner city and would remain flammable indefinitely.

The black community, like others, is fragmented in so many ways. It is split by class and status, education, values, religion, and history. However, for reasons stemming from our history in this country that is distinctly ours, we also differ on what direction we should collectively pursue. We can't even agree on the notion that we are a united people capable of collective action. Furthermore, instead of seeing ourselves as a beautiful collection of different hues—as autumn leaves are—we often disturbingly make separations, distinctions, and perceptions based on skin color and hair texture.

One thing that *can* galvanize the black community is the positive goodwill, support, hope, and success for our young athletes. It doesn't matter whether we are casual fans or card-carrying sports fanatics, we are proud of the athletic success of our youth when they persevere and reach prominence as adults in their chosen sports.

In spite of the great pride, unity, and hope held by the black community, the infusion of athletic shoe company money altered our youth sports infrastructure. All of the sudden, like a glass shattering on the floor in every direction, a kind of youth sports anarchy broke out. In Washington, DC, in the middle 1980s, everybody and everything associated with spring and summer basketball was under suspicion. Distrust was the order of the day as people built empires, carried out hidden agendas, and waged turf wars to determine who was in charge.

Furthermore, to the dismay of many, there were folk making judgments about the potential and talent of young athletes who had no expertise to do so. This happened due to the shortsightedness of the athletic shoe companies. Neither they nor AAU and the other purveyors of spring and summer basketball did background checks, criminal or otherwise, on the adult leaders who made themselves available. It seemed that the selection process did not go any deeper than the word-of-mouth recommendation from a coach or street agent who previously "delivered" a player to a school, or supposedly had ties and access to players, or was supposedly deeply involved in working with youth in the community.

Nobody knew for sure the kind of résumé that would attract an athletic shoe company sponsorship. Was it just the ability to corral the best players? Was it the ability to coach, handle money, build, and maintain a grassroots organization, or all of the above?

There was an array of different men and women leading teams from the sidelines, including former college players, former coaches, former local high school stars that, for various reasons, could not make it on the college level, old timers who had always been around the game but their actual occupation was never clear, former street ballers who had troubles with the law, parents of players on the team, and a new wave of people that left you to wonder exactly why they were involved in youth sports. Consequently, adult leadership was looked on with distrust, disregard, and even contempt. Everyone questioned their association and searched for their motives and agendas within the newfound union of shoe sponsored teams, AAU, and competitive travel basketball.

Beyond questions about the adult leadership were the doubts about how AAU was organized. Things were moving fast. Although AAU had the blueprint and know-how to structure this level of youth basketball, it appeared that its national management was ill-prepared for the sheer intensity, passion, and devotion of city youth basketball.

Rules and guidelines for local tournaments at various levels seemed to change constantly, certainly season to season if not week to week. Teams made protests that sometimes went from the regional level supposedly all the way to corporate in Florida for resolution. Qualifying tournaments were hastily added. Age brackets were altered; team pairings and matchups in tournaments were sometimes readjusted at game time. Some games were replayed; others were declared a forfeit. Entire teams were kicked out of qualifying tournaments.

The team credentials, memberships, and birth certificates of players were constantly in question and challenged. The birth certificate flap was a big problem. Team coaches had to prove the age of players to compete in a tournament at check-in before a game. Often a birth certificate was provided by coach

& player to tournament administrators at the game site to verify the player was participating in the proper age bracket. But as gym sites changed so did the administrators and often the inspection process. The lack of cohesion and communication between gyms caused confusion for all. Sadly, many adult leaders pounced and had no problem with playing loose with the rules. More than once I witnessed a coach handing a player who was too old to play in a particular age bracket a doctored ID or certificate to beat the system. The youngsters were under twelve years old. A horrendously poor example of teaching the positive virtues of sport!

The reasons for this administrative implosion were multi-faceted. The AAU organization, specifically at the local level in the DC region, seemed disorganized and caught off guard by the onslaught. New opportunities to make money were unfolding daily, it seemed. For example, every player had to get an AAU membership card from corporate headquarters, but it essentially meant nothing as it related to actual verification of a player's status regarding who he was or his age. It merely provided entry into AAU events.

Many people put in positions of leadership and accountability at the regional and local levels were incompetent or in it solely for the money. Others who volunteered their services and time for the benefit of youth, but who may have lacked organizational and event management skills, would simply quit when faced with hostility from other adults and parents.

Blueprint for Success

As with any good and profitable idea, there soon were other companies sponsoring youth basketball in the inner city. If Nike's model was successful, wouldn't one expect Converse,

Adidas, Reebok, and Under Armor to replicate it? This is not exclusive to corporate America.

Consequently, in the inner city the toxic mix of youth, basketball, and money—aided by dysfunction in leadership— spawned a new contingent of grassroots sports entrepreneurs. The youth sports community saw the benefits of playing on shoe-sponsored teams. The athletic shoe companies saw an army of players' wide-eyed interest and bouncing exuberance and eagerness to play.

More importantly, grassroots sports entrepreneurs saw parents unfamiliar to youth sports who could be duped into believing that AAU and competitive travel basketball formed the yellow-brick road to athletic scholarship. These parents were thus willing to "pay to play" for their athletes' future success.

Veteran coaches of high school teams saw this scenario play out in the early days of the movement to sponsor travel basketball in the black community and were awestruck by the adult leaders' stampede. These coaches can recall an introduction meeting to Potomac Valley AAU, the local AAU chapter serving the DC region, where more than 250 prospective adult team leaders showed for orientation to AAU youth basketball. Prince George's County was and is an extremely enticing place to establish an AAU youth basketball program. With a predominately black population hooked on hoops and known as one of the wealthiest black counties in the nation, opportunities for making money selling basketball dreams were abundant.

Suddenly, a legion of grassroots teams was formed. This was a good thing on the surface as young athletes wanting to play AAU basketball were given a chance to play, while excited parents wanting to maximize the potential of their athletes had the financial wherewithal to enable them to play.

But not so fast. Once again, the powers that be tricked the black youth sports community.

Everyone wanted to know the motivations of these grassroots team leaders and coaches. Was the program about money first and progress of young athletes second? The only thing that parents knew for sure was that there were plentiful teams to choose from.

The parents were right to be suspicious. Many of the adult leaders were indeed out to make money. Others were motivated to land a college coaching opportunity by delivering a star recruit into the right hands. Those out to make money no longer saw young athletes for the promise of their future success, but instead as commodities or product. Parents were viewed as clients, and the basketball dream was the service provided. True to form, these adult leaders and coaches would say the appropriate clichés, all the right things about "maximizing youth athletic potential" or "providing exposure to scholarship opportunities" or "teaching youth the values and lessons inherent in sports participation," but their actions spoke another language, a lingo displaying the art of the hustle. The proof was in subtle and not-so-subtle practices:

• Charging $25 per player for two-day tryouts with rosters that were 95 percent established.
• Charging excessive and exorbitant memberships fees and dues to participate and play on a team.
• Charging parents top dollar to purchase uniforms and sneakers.
• Organizing fundraising ventures that required athletes and parents to participate, such as car washes, raffles, and

donut sales, yet failing to share or report the proceeds with the parents.

• Having long rosters of fourteen or fifteen players simply because parents would pay to play. Yet playing time would be the last thing some players would receive on rosters that deep.

• Sponsoring tournaments with excessive entry fees and overpriced concessions, while using parents to "volunteer" their time to sell and collect money at the door, or work the scorebook and clock, all the while cutting corners on gym safety and especially refusing to pay for competent and quality referees.

All of these were telltale signs that deep oversight was needed by parents before signing their athlete to a grassroots team. But due to the frenzy started by the introduction of athletic shoe-company money into black youth sports, the runaway sports-dream train was rolling downhill without brakes.

Recruitment

The selection process of young athletes easily ensured that the black youth sports community was headed for big problems. Who were these people heading up this new venture called AAU and what were their credentials to decide who could play basketball and who couldn't?

Player movement seemed free and easy. For any reason, a player could quit one team on Friday and suit up with another team playing in a different tournament on Saturday. Coaches and team adult leaders would recruit players callously and blatantly, even making direct pitches to athletes on opposing teams and their parents at the end of a game. Parents would go back on their word, retract their commitment to a particular team, and move their athlete for what they presumed were greener athletic pastures that promised more opportunities to have their child exposed to college recruiters.

Young athletes would abandon teams for any number of vague reasons, from lack of playing time or a disagreement with the coach to wanting to play another position that their entourage deemed best. Other arbitrary and simplistic rationales included uniform colors and the supposed reputations of certain teams based on whether or not they were sponsored by an athletic shoe company. Soon there were monetary enticements to join a team. Athletic gear and sneakers were standard negotiating chips in the decision-making process.

Since this was youth basketball and a cherished segment of sports in the black community, this infighting for players was dealt with through many forms of retribution. Often shouting matches could be heard after games between team coaches and adult leaders. On more than one occasion, accusations led to punches. On one particular spring night, words were never exchanged: one coach simply walked up to another after a game and knocked him unconscious.

Selective Coaching

With recruiting an open-market affair, some coaches felt they needed to be 24/7 watchdogs to protect their players from the talent poachers around the game. Yet, they mistakenly would make other concessions to these same star players. For instance, they would pacify them, essentially allowing a hoops prodigy to do as he pleased on the court for fear of alienating him and his parents, thus hastening his possible exodus to another team.

This turn-the-other-cheek coaching style happened quite frequently in AAU and competitive travel basketball programs, and it still happens today. In truth, it has been an issue for some time in high school and youth sports. When a coach realizes he has an exceptional talent on his team, in order to win he makes concessions to that player. In basketball this includes ignoring on-court transgressions such as selfishness, poor fundamentals, emotional outbursts, and obvious disdain toward adult leaders such as referees and assistant coaches. However, in AAU and competitive travel basketball recruiting and backroom deals for players happen quickly, and as parents' egos and self-centered motivations combine with the whimsy of spoiled athletic prodigies, many intimidated coaches often look the other way or even shun their coaching responsibilities altogether.

Of course, among the reasons these coaches evade confrontations with young players is because they themselves have ulterior motives. They may see the player as their key to moving up the AAU food chain of coaching opportunities and getting a high school position or even better a college assistant job. They know that in order to keep (or get) shoe-money sponsorships and the healthy incomes they provide, they must continue to send athletes to colleges. The sponsorships certainly will dry up quickly if programs are not winning and getting exposure nationally, because the athletic shoe companies are not trying to support programs that remain neighborhood or sincere grassroots entities.

Coaches may have a multitude of agendas; however, the bottom line is they look the other way when working with their star players. Ultimately it is a total disservice to players because the authority structure is uprooted. Players (and parents) gain a sense of entitlement and a false perception of what basketball will hold for them. This is especially detrimental in the black community because black athletes, celebrated for their basketball prowess, already are given high pedestal status. Yet some coaches in AAU and competitive travel basketball join in the adulation with praise instead of discipline, compliments instead of correction, and compliance instead of teaching the fundamentals. Sadly, this forfeiture of coaching duties happens with players just twelve or even younger, when they should not only be receiving quality instruction on fundamentals but also on discipline, sportsmanship, and respect for himself, others, and especially the game of basketball.

This AAU scenario is repeated each and every season. In fact, in speaking with adult leaders with deep AAU basketball experience, I have learned the only debate is over the percentage of coaches who placate players, not the fact that it happens.

Joe Hampton is a perfect case study of this failure in discipline. He was a man child at age twelve. The talented basketball player already stood 6 feet, 4 inches with a good body and basketball frame that said he was far from reaching his last growth spurt. His skills were clearly more advanced than those of other players his age, and definitely for a youngster his size. He handled the ball on the perimeter and in the open court like a guard and also exhibited a comfortable shooting range from the three-point line. Add to this package a high basketball IQ and, noteworthy, he was a lefty—an advantage in a right-hand dominant game. Next-level success for Joe, which would have been high school hoops, was assured. The questions started with how high his climb on the Sports Pyramid, how "great" he could become.

Chapter 2: The Tricky Relationship between AAU Basketball and the Black Sports Community

Joe played for Force One, a local AAU grassroots program from Silver Spring, Maryland, in Montgomery County outside Washington, DC. The program was without shoe sponsor money. He was coached by Steven Depollar, who like many AAU and travel basketball coaches founded the program and, with a son of his own who played, was motivated to compete. Many in the AAU culture predicted that soon the big boys of AAU, the shoe-sponsored programs featuring AAU city powers DC Assault and Team Takeover, would come a-calling and Joe would surely leave. As a referee for some of Joe's games and spectator on others, I knew this would happen quickly. Whether Depollar knew this and believed he could stem the tide didn't really matter. What was evident was that Joe was accorded "star treatment."

A referee has a good vantage point to evaluate if good coaching is taking place. He sees the intricacies of coaching on display as well as the interaction between coach and player. I saw that Depollar knew the game. He would bark at other players for mental lapses and physical errors. He would call out plays and substitute frequently according to how players' skills fit into his game plan. He questioned referee calls with knowledge of the rule book.

Under Depollar, Joe had free rein to do as he pleased. He shot the ball when he wanted from wherever he wanted. He would bring the ball down the floor, looking off the ball-handling guards and creating his own plays that eschewed the team's offense. Worse yet, Joe would take plays off, get lazy on defense, and complain to the referees. Clearly, Depollar was aware and knew this behavior was wrong, but he allowed Joe to get away with it. He held the other players accountable but not Joe.

Whether Depollar was unaware of Joe's poor habits or ignored them to pacify him really did not matter when it came to Joe's progress as a basketball player. Either way Joe was in a bad situation. He wasn't being taught the game properly, nor was he given proper guidance to mature as a young man through basketball. Despite his potential, his growth was being restricted. For his own good, he needed to leave the program.

Joe and his father joined DC Assault. Joe was fortunate to be coached in the thirteen and under age bracket by Zack Suber, a former college coach who would not appease him. Joe enrolled at famed DeMatha Catholic High School and played varsity as a freshman under the tutelage of another knowledgeable and tough-love coach, Mike Jones.

On another occasion an AAU recruit came to Coach Reese's grassroots program and complained that his former coach told another teammate to shoot the ball every time he touched it. Unsure of the authenticity of the remark and knowing the coach, I asked him if this was true. The coach confirmed it was, adding that the player's passing skills and decision-making were so poor that he preferred the player shoot the ball instead of throwing it away in the stands.

This is the sports equivalent to rewarding a child who refuses to eat his or her vegetables during dinner with cake and ice cream. Once again, the bottom line here is failing to teach proper fundamentals and abdicating one's responsibilities as coach.

Yet another issue, and one that raises critical questions about AAU and competitive travel basketball and other sports as well, is its exclusivity. Many young athletes are excluded from participating solely because they cannot pay to play. AAU and competitive travel basketball are costly endeavors. A lot of players with talent, heart, and determination don't get the chance to play because their parents or guardians simply can't make the financial obligations—the fees, dues, transportation to and from practice and games, lodging for out-of-town trips, and more.

The extremely talented athletes in these money-tight situations do not have these problems. The shoe-sponsored teams or other sponsored programs absorb the athletes' costs. However, many other talented players capable of excelling if given a chance are left totally out of the entire process.

Many black team coaches and adult program leaders are nonetheless unrepentant about excluding players for financial reasons. Despite running grassroots organizations and being armed, in many cases, with a nonprofit classification and mission statement to serve their youth communities, these leaders will proudly and loudly say without hesitation that they do not recruit players in certain parts of the city, perhaps only a fifteen-minute ride away from their program headquarters, merely because they have pigeonholed players (along with their parents) as "non-payers." These black men see no need in reaching out of their comfort zones. Instead they remain in the fertile neighborhoods, those lush reservoirs of black youth and parents with hefty checkbooks, thus paying the way for their own hoop dreams.

Chapter 3: The Scholarship Dream: Do You Really Know What You're Chasing?

There are many distressing facets of AAU and competitive travel basketball within the black youth sports community. What is most unsettling and painful is how impulsively many black parents decide to enlist their children in programs. Too often it's a knee-jerk, desperate decision made without any preparation, background information, research, or homework. The parents are so infatuated with sports, specifically basketball, that many simply can find no fault with the process. They are completely sold on AAU and competitive travel basketball and what these programs can provide for them and their athlete. They have little or no knowledge of what precisely they hope to accomplish or what it really entails or how difficult the journey will be.

They think they know. When asked they respond with the obligatory, "I want my child to get exposure to college coaches and get an athletic scholarship." That sounds like a logical and appropriate reply, but it really only displays how AAU participation has conditioned these parents. It is a mindset shaped by a myriad of factors that include:

1. The black sports community's infatuation with basketball and arrogance that it is "our game," that we have some type of patent or exclusivity to succeed in the sport.

2. The ease with which their child and sports knowledgeable people recite the names of athletes, both local and national, who have reached next-level Sports Pyramid, athlete success (e.g., a college scholarship or an NBA contract)

31

supposedly through their participation in AAU and competitive travel basketball.

3.   The distrust of the neighborhood high school's athletic program. The community often believes that local schools will ultimately restrict athletes from getting a "good look" from colleges. Skeptics cite the lack of success of the school's teams, the alleged deficiency of quality coaching and support, and the lack of players who have advanced to the next level. Ironically, this is one of the few points on which black communities agree since this perspective has no geographical or socioeconomic boundaries. Often black parents in suburbia as well as in urban centers feel there are fewer athletic scholarship opportunities for their child at the neighborhood school, and thus they feel compelled to have the child compete in AAU and competitive travel basketball.

4.   The slick marketing of the billion-dollar youth sports industry, combined with the monies from the athletic shoe companies. The combination has overwhelmed adults within the black youth sports community into believing that participation in AAU and competitive travel basketball is a must, and failure to do so makes one an inadequate parent. The guilt trip that comes with not participating can be agonizing.

Even when black parents acknowledge this quartet of factors, they still feel that registering their child in AAU and competitive travel basketball will provide enhanced scholarship opportunities. After all, who can criticize parents who are trying to provide every opportunity for their children to reach their dreams and goals? Who dare pass judgment on parents who are sacrificing for the betterment of their children?

So these parents become prideful and defensive and immediately rebel at any suggestion that their decision is not the cure-all answer. They see the questioner as an interloper or second guesser passing judgment on them as parents. They do not make a distinction between a discussion that is founded on sound knowledge of youth sports and one that is not. Instead, *they* are the ones who are armed with logic and rationality. Thanks to slick marketing and legions of dream sellers, they believe that the AAU is the only option, or at least the best one they can make given their situation. This misunderstanding leads to friction between parents and other adult leaders.

It is largely a matter of parents failing to seek out information that could assist them and their child in reaching their sports dreams that is concerning. While parents and adult leadership calmly and reflexively say that AAU participation is about "expanding opportunities" for their child, often their behavior and actions illustrate a desperation and all-consuming addiction to the sport. Examples abound of this conduct:

1.   During games parents are hostile and rush to criticize the AAU coach and leadership, definitely the referees, and perhaps even the players, including their own child who may be as young as eight or nine years old. These parents scream, holler, curse, make idle threats, and are far more frenzied and engaged than what, say, winning a fifth grade or 11 & Under game merits, a weekend contest that will have very little value and memory come Monday.

2.   Parents and others frequently refer to how a talented athlete "is going to be good." The emphasis is not on the current reality—that the athlete right now is a fine player at age ten or twelve or fifteen—but how good he will be in the

future. This rush to tag players this way illustrates that AAU and competitive travel basketball is often about projection and potential, not the enjoyment of the moment. It speaks to the intense pressure on the athlete to continuously perform.

3. Parents forfeit personal and family time and financial resources. Many black parents see it as their duty to block out every weekend from April through the end of July for AAU and competitive travel basketball, either for local tournaments or tournaments in other cities. (This does not include time for practices, which generally take place two to three times each week). The time and financial resources that are required are unquestioned and given without constraint as these parents are locked-n-loaded on the notion that their athletic scholarship dreams demand that level of sacrifice. In essence, this is yet another ruse within black youth sports that disrupts the family structure. Several important holidays and other events are compromised, reduced, neglected or celebrated on the fly, including Easter Sunday, Mother's Day, Father's Day, Memorial Day, Fourth of July, school proms, and graduations for other siblings. For these important family occasions to compete against the competitive travel basketball slate is ludicrous and speaks to misplaced family values.

Can the Same Be Said for Club and Travel Sports in the Suburbs?

A fair question to be asked is what makes the AAU basketball experience for the predominantly black urban community so different from the experiences of the predominantly white and suburban communities involved in club and travel sports like soccer, hockey, and volleyball. Indeed, participation in club and travel team soccer and volleyball is just as grueling, time-consuming, extremely expensive and family-unfriendly as basketball is in the black community. In fact, there are far more similarities than differences as most regard club and travel teams as the same, just under a different moniker.

While the intensity and commitment are the same, there are a few sociological and philosophical differences at play. First and foremost, because there are substantially fewer two-parent households in the black community than there are in suburban and white communities, there is the obvious issue regarding income and finances. By comparison, children in suburban and white households benefit from higher expectations in life whether they participate in sports or not. There is generally less pressure in these communities to compete in sports. Conversely, in the black community, financial problems and the lack of upward mobility options force the idea that the basketball scholarship is the only ticket to better living. Thus, the pressures to excel magnify, and the desperation for a scholarship is palpable.

Meanwhile, suburban club and travel team athletes do not believe that their athletic performance is the *only* path to higher education and attending college. They have the freedom to play for enjoyment and pleasure, improvement and learning, recreation and exercise. They have the luxury to compete in the moment and not be burdened with the expectations for tomorrow. Not everyone has this luxury in these communities, but certainly a far greater number than inner city athletes. Clearly the main distinction between travel and club sports that are popular in the suburbs and AAU and competitive travel basketball participation in the city is the unyielding faith the black community has that basketball is a panacea. The suburban, predominantly white community has no such faith nor a relationship to a sport that ultimately devours more of its young than it promotes.

Valentine's Day

The trusting and faith promise that basketball will always deliver in the black community was on full display in the winter of 2014. In Prince Georges County MD just outside the DC city line during the month of February, earlier than the normal AAU and competitive travel basketball played in the spring and summer season usually starting in April, the Maryland Invitational Tournament (MIT) is put on by proprietor Gary Pinkney.

The February event is for boys' teams with players from second to eighth grade. Teams from all over the country come to participate. It is a well respected and well organized event, expertly led by Pinkney since its inception in 1994. The facilities are top shelf, the event adult leadership is thorough, and Pinkney has quality referees on the courts and well-informed administrators at the score tables. The 2014 entry fee was $390.00 per team. Despite a Valentine's Day snowstorm that postponed the event for a week, Pinkney told me he still had 113 teams in the tournament. As the referee working the three-day event, I saw roughly only eight to ten teams with white adult leadership and mostly white athletes on the court. Easily more than 100 teams in the event featured predominately black rosters with black adult leadership. This is a clear example of the black community's overly dependent or, perhaps, hypnotic reliance on basketball.

A Basketball Love Affair

Basketball in the black community is omnipresent at all levels—youth, scholastic, and scholarship. Hoop dreams in the black sports community is a hand-in-glove fit, just as the Bible is to the church. We, in the black sports community have a blind trust and faith that sports, specifically basketball, will lead us to a better lot in life. Basketball has become our identity, our name, our status. The game goes far deeper than being what we do and has morphed into who we are. The game is played with purpose, pride, and soul. To play the game is to put your existence on display. It is not played flippantly, but for short-term gratification and pride as well as long-term prospects of providing for a better day. Traditional paths to a top-quality lifestyle—school, college, a good job—pale in comparison to the promise of a happier tomorrow that basketball (NBA) offers.

Yet the reciprocity most players seek *from* basketball is obviously never as strong. Basketball will never return the respect, devotion, love, and lifelong commitment that the black athlete brings to the game. It can't. The sheer numbers vying for its affection ensure it. The Sports Pyramid demands it. Basketball is a sport that is for the young but never ages itself. Yet due to our unconditional love and blind devotion, we are often ill-prepared for that sudden jilting. We have not prepared an alternative plan, a second dream, if you will. We have not found anything that can touch our hearts or even provide us sustenance like the game of basketball.

If one wants to see a sports Darwinism "survival of the fittest" phenomenon in effect, they need only travel through the black sports community, its basketball community in particular. One of the primary, yet not usually discussed, reasons why young black athletes do not compete in large numbers in other sports (lacrosse, soccer, baseball, etc.) is the all-out manpower and energy that is wedded to "making it" solely through basketball and football. Through this sports struggle, a select group of black sports champions are produced and those players subsequently leave the community to go on and dominate the professional sports landscapes of the NBA and NFL. Many good, talented, multi-skilled athletes remain behind. They do not make it to the top of the hoops pyramid, and since they have invested the lion's share of time, energy, and service to basketball, they no longer have the inclination or desire to re-train in another sport even though, given their athletic gifts and mental toughness, they certainly could excel if they pursued them.

This is what makes AAU and competitive travel basketball, working in conjunction with the athletic shoe companies' sponsorships, so manipulative. These programs glorify and intensify our obsessive, one-way relationship with the sport. They perpetuate our belief that the sport is our domain, and we are entitled to success. They give the community added confidence and license to believe that our faith in the sport is healthy, thriving, and beneficial. Instead of questioning why athletic shoe company money rolled into the community, or why we should turn our family values inside out, chasing basketball dreams, or why we send our athletes (starting at age eight or younger) on a confining, blinders-on, one-way trek without an alternate plan, a second dream we simply rejoice in our narrow-thinking comfort zone, trusting basketball as our sports salvation.

Furthermore, AAU, other purveyors of competitive travel basketball, and the athletic shoe companies are pursuing our athletes on the cheap. Like dandelions growing on the lawn, they descend each spring into our neighborhood gyms, selling basketball dreams in one hand while lifting our cash-light wallets with the other. That last dollar of ours they're taking should be spent toward needed recreation resources for our youth.

This annual spring-to-summer poaching of our young athletes' dreams, our time, our fleeting personal discretionary (or often monthly bill-allocated) monies, and community resources is allowed to happen in the black community for one primary reason: simply put, basketball—youth basketball in the black community—is religion, and these mostly white, dream-selling entrepreneurs promoting AAU and competitive travel basketball are our pastors and storefront preachers, while we, the merciful, dutiful, and trusting youth sports congregation, are dropping our last dollars and coins into the offering plate, believing that sermon about athletic scholarship and prosperity. Consequently, as we are swept up in the emotional praise and worship of more opportunities to play and serve our Lady of Basketball Dreams, we don't bother to question, think critically, or hold anyone accountable to the words they preach.

Furthermore, and this is the kicker, how many players actually receive scholarships exclusively due to their participation in AAU and competitive travel basketball? There is no way to provide an accurate count. For all the grandiose proclamations about the waves of five-star recruits who play AAU each season, the fact remains that these are the kinds of athletes who are targeted for scholarships regardless. They are extremely productive players that dominate on their high school teams. These talented athletes are often playing AAU and competitive travel basketball merely for street credentials, reputation, competition, tout-sheet rankings or the fancy of a bigger college hoops program. They have scholarship offers in hand and do not need AAU.

Chapter 3: The Scholarship Dream: Do You Really Know What You're Chasing?

For every athlete who says AAU was the key to getting a basketball scholarship, I can list dozens who did not obtain an athletic offer from a college nor gather any introductory letters of interest from a college basketball program. And this is from many athletes who competed in AAU and competitive travel basketball since age ten or younger. Moreover, the NCAA, for a multitude of reasons, including wanting to take recruiting influence away from AAU and other travel basketball coaches, has restricted the number of times Division I coaches can leave campus and watch high school athletes compete in AAU tournaments and similar competitions. In 2014, this "open period" lasted for roughly a few weeks of the five months that constitute the spring and summer basketball season.

All other tournaments occur during the "dead period," the time when Division I coaches are restricted from AAU and competitive travel basketball games. These tournaments are in essence glorified practice games, albeit making for good competition, similar to NFL pre-season games. Consequently, all the sacrifices and costs, financial or otherwise, that families make, are mostly for the sake of competition and neighborhood or city pride. Again, here is the trick: AAU and competitive travel basketball should be about competition and improving your skills, the events' most redeeming benefits as tournaments are very spirited and intense. However, among many black parents, adult leaders, and black players, the first priority is not for these benefits but getting a scholarship. It is a humongous case of misplaced, incorrect priorities. The goal for an athlete should be to improve his game, and as a result, the interest of recruiters and colleges may naturally follow.

There is an old adage regarding recruiting in sports that says, "If you can play, they (the college recruiters) will find you." With advances in social media today, the statement is more valid than ever before. Yes, AAU and competitive travel basketball provide opportunities for large numbers of Division I coaches to watch players in competitive environments, but only at selected times, not the entire spring and summer season. Furthermore, where is the concrete evidence that AAU basketball is the preeminent venue where scholarship deals are forged? The scholarship reward from competing in AAU and competitive travel basketball can't be tracked in that way. There is no accountability.

Yet, in truth it doesn't really matter. Many in the black sports community have been cautioned about the false promises of AAU and competitive travel basketball participation. And by and large, the community still wants to believe in the pipe dream that AAU is selling. So it does. After all, AAU and competitive travel basketball, at the least, provide another opportunity for the black sports community to romance and dance with its first love.

The Lottery
The ease with which many black parents believe that basketball is the light is very disconcerting. Their lack of knowledge is not the problem rather, they don't seek that knowledge. The young athletes deserve a pass. They are merely following the lead of the adults. They want to play. Their peers play. They see and know personally many of the stars at the next level of college or even the NBA who have played AAU hoops. Their minds have been captivated by the glitzy marketing and ESPN reports of college scholarship

success through AAU. Thus, their desire to compete is understandable.

But for black parents and other adult leaders, to fall prey so easily to the same blitz of information makes one cringe. Furthermore, many seem to make no attempt whatsoever to educate themselves. They encase themselves in the mindset that "this is basketball" and this is a path that we, the black sports community, travel, so it must be acceptable and beneficial. It seems that parents do more homework when buying a new flat screen TV than pursuing a basketball scholarship for their child. They are content in their naiveté, and they blindly trust the process. It can only be called what it is: a disservice to young athletes.

First, there is a misconception within the black sports community that an athletic scholarship is an entitlement, a low-hanging fruit waiting to be plucked once an athlete is placed in the right environment, such as an AAU program. This is wrong. Where does this belief come from?

Surely, it cannot come from a clear look within the sports community. That will reveal the obvious, that only 0.03 percent of scholastic athletes will play at the collegiate level after high school according to NCAA data.

Perhaps this false perception of the numbers comes from watching black athletes dominate the courts and playing fields in the NBA and NFL, as well as in big-time Division I (D-I) basketball and football.

According to data provided by the 2013 Racial and Gender Report Card, in the 2012 season, black athletes made up 76.3 percent of all NBA players and 66.3 percent of NFL players, respectively.

Meanwhile, to further extend the eye test of black athletic participation at the college level, a recent University of

Pennsylvania study showed that 64 percent of basketball players and 57 percent of football players in the six powerhouse college conferences in the United States were black men. The conferences studied included the Atlantic Coast Conference (ACC), Big East Conference, Big Ten Conference, Big 12 Conference, Pac 12 Conference, and the Southeastern Conference (SEC).

Whatever the criteria used, it's shortsighted and unsubstantiated to assume that receiving an athletic scholarship is easy. Getting a basketball scholarship to continue your athletic career is a magnificent opportunity that, according to NCAA data, only 3.3 percent of all high school athletes achieve.

The NCAA has many roads offering athletic scholarships—D-I, D-II, D-III (the latter being a financial package, not a scholarship). There are similar opportunities through separate collegiate bodies such as the NAIA and JUCO (junior colleges). But let's be clear, most parents and athletes misguidedly pursue the more visible ESPN-televised, *SportsCenter*-highlight-grabbing stepping stone to the NBA and NFL opportunity that is the Division I scholarship.

Fine, it's good to set those goals high, but let's look at some numbers that involve just Division I men's basketball. In 2013, there were 351 schools competing at the D-I level that offered 13 men's scholarships. During a given season, most schools generally will make available between three and six scholarships after graduations and transfers. If we generously assign five available scholarships per school in D-I men's basketball, that amounts to a total of 1,755 available scholarships per season. According to data published by the NCAA, approximately 538,000 youth play high school basketball in this country. That's roughly a 1 in 307 chance of landing a D-I men's athletic scholarship. Now, let's assume that in order to acquire a D-I scholarship a player must be among the starting five on his team. The math reveals that is one player getting a Division I basketball scholarship out of every sixty-one high schools playing the sport.

Obviously, you can do many creative things with statistics, but black parents need to be aware, alert, and definitely devoid of misperceptions. I am not implying here that the black athlete should not seek a basketball scholarship because the odds are long. Black families and black youth are accustomed to overcoming long odds in almost all societal endeavors. However, a lack of knowledge is not an excuse.

Parents should use AAU basketball as a potential resource, reference, and tool to assist them as they pursue athletic scholarship opportunities. To acquire a basketball scholarship, black parents and adult leaders should not have all their eggs in one basket, a practice deriving from the desperate belief that AAU and competitive travel basketball is the exclusive answer.

Chapter 4: All That Glitters Is Not AAU Gold

For many, AAU basketball is synonymous with all spring and summer youth basketball. This is a point of confusion with serious implications.

In today's youth sports culture, almost all spring and summer youth basketball is incorrectly labeled "AAU basketball." Young athletes, eager to participate and play, swell with pride when telling all they are playing AAU basketball. Adult men and women stand tall when they are addressed as AAU coaches. Teams and organizations boldly attach the acronym to their names for the status and positive associations of the AAU brand. Tournament hosts and organizers capitalize on the name for profit, reputation, marketing, hype, respect, and acceptance within youth sports.

Entire sports communities, specifically the black community, blindly give their trust and honor to what they believe is the pinnacle of youth sport participation. In doing so, the community bestows privilege and distinction to its young athletes, as well as promise to the name.

This misconception exists because all who participate within it—sports community leaders, adults and parents, dream-selling entrepreneurs, and young athletes—see personal financial gain, favor, and advantage in maintaining the status quo of AAU basketball.

Even AAU's leadership at national headquarters in Lake Buena Vista, Florida, aren't worried about clearing up the fallacy that all youth basketball played during the spring and summer season is licensed or sanctioned by the AAU. Nor is it anxious to take legal action against all the sports entities that use its name unknowingly or purposely for gain without the organization's permission. In fact, AAU headquarters concedes that it can't take action against all those who use its name. It is too extensive a project to catch everyone. All this reveals that the AAU basketball brand is clearly entrenched in the youth sports culture.

AAU, it seems, accepts the marketing principle that all publicity, even the bad kind, is indeed good publicity. And the company's point is valid. AAU basketball has cornered the youth hoops market and is recognized as the elite of athletic competition.

The official history of AAU, available on its website (www.aausports.org), describes the organization's legacy:

The Amateur Athletic Union (AAU) is one of the largest, non-profit, volunteer, sports organizations in the United States. A multi-sport organization, the AAU is dedicated exclusively to the promotion and development of amateur sports and physical fitness programs.

The AAU was founded in 1888 to establish standards and uniformity in amateur sports. During its early years, the AAU served as a leader in international sport representing the United States in the international sports federations. The AAU worked closely with the Olympic movement to prepare athletes for the Olympic Games. After the Amateur Sports Act of 1978, the AAU has focused its efforts into providing sports programs for all participants of all ages beginning at the grass roots level.

With over 125 years of service in sports and despite having competitions in over thirty-five other sports, no sport has the prestige and popularity of spring and summer basketball. Unlike those other sports, basketball is not labeled a "travel" sport. Indeed, it should be tagged as such, but youth basketball, thanks to Sonny Vaccaro, Nike and the turmoil the NCAA spawns, has given AAU a basketball identity, a brand and household name that supersedes all connections with other sports. AAU basketball is to spring and summer youth hoops what Kleenex is to tissue.

From a business standpoint this makes good sense. Every hit to its website is another advertising and marketing opportunity, another way to acquire a new customer. AAU need not apologize or seek to separate itself from all the imitators and perpetrators that take advantage of unsuspecting participants. As with any purchase, "Let the buyer beware."

However, what is transpiring now, as youth sports has mushroomed into a multi-billion-dollar annual industry, is that greedy and cunning dream-selling entrepreneurs are using the AAU basketball label to hijack the hopes, wallets, and spirits of uninformed parents and their athletes.

Clarity is needed. Fundamental information needs to be circulated. Too many participants within the youth basketball culture are being misled and bamboozled by perpetrators using the AAU tag.

An example that immediately comes to mind is the promotion of various tournaments as "AAU licensed" events. An AAU event is licensed only if it is advertised and listed on its website. That is it. Period. Case closed. Any other event listed as AAU "licensed" or "sanctioned" (an older label the organization and imitations used) is false advertising.

This distinction is an important one because many players and their families bend over backwards and make rash decisions to transfer from team to team or league to league in pursuit of unlicensed AAU programs that are really AAU in name only.

Chapter 4: All That Glitters Is Not AAU Gold

AAU is commonly accused of false advertising, and while it is "at the scene of the crime" in terms of benefiting from broad associations with spring and summer basketball programs, in its defense AAU does clearly state on its website the criteria to be an official AAU member.

This brings up another official sounding phrase flippantly being tossed around to describe events: "NCAA certified." For spring and summer basketball events, simply stated, NCAA certification applies to situations where the NCAA allows Division I coaches to attend events such as AAU national tournaments or showcase events, all-star games, and elite camps. There the coaches recruit and evaluate prospective athletes, which is only permitted during this relatively short "open period." In 2014, the open or evaluation period was one weekend in April and three weeks in July. All other dates in the spring and summer months were classified as "quiet" or "dead" periods and restricted coaches from having contact with recruitable athletes.

What does this mean for the athletes competing in spring and summer basketball? In 2014, on-the-court opportunities to impress coaches for those highly coveted D-I scholarships only happened within a total of 18 days spread out between late March and the end of July. With these restrictions in mind, when parents share with me their child's AAU season schedule, filled with almost weekly events, I wonder what goals they and the program leaders are really trying to accomplish.

A complex system of rules, and more pivotally, a convenient wink-wink association between AAU basketball and other purveyors of spring and summer travel basketball are responsible for a lot of the confusion parents and participants experience. The chummy relationship benefits both AAU and the purveyors while leaving adults, including many naïve but well-intentioned coaches and parents, perplexed and susceptible to blindly buy into dream-selling schemes.

When AAU Became King

AAU did not always have such a strong brand in the inner city. For much of its 125-year existence, the urban sports community viewed AAU as a nice, alternate, off-season sporting outlet for predominately affluent and white youth. The organization was devoid of a basketball stronghold in the inner city, where AAU was more associated with track and field. For example, in the 1970s, for young basketball players living in Washington, DC, and other cities, the off-season goal was to compete in all-star inter-city events such as the Youth Games and Boston Shootout, or compete in one of the then-novel but burgeoning high school all-star games or invitation-only basketball camps. These events were the precursors of the AAU-sponsored events of today.

The most popular alternatives to the all-star teams or camps were the prestigious summer leagues such as the Jelleff League in Washington, DC, the Sonny Hill League in Philadelphia, or the Rucker League in New York. These esteemed summer leagues were mostly played outdoors, unbelievable as it may seem today where youth basketball players compete in temperature-controlled, well-lit, shining, waxed-and-buffed, neatly lined floors with LED-blazoned scoreboards in sports complexes with ten or more courts.

Contrast these state-of-the-art complexes with the hard asphalt courts of those past days, often uneven and rarely level, hoops with chipped orange paint and bent rims, sections of net missing or dangling (if the nets were rope and not chain link), and poles barely ten feet tall. Usually the games started in the early evening and ran into the night, but the humidity of those east coast summers never seemed to subside. If you played the early evening games, another defender could be the setting sun behind your basket, creating more havoc on your shooting accuracy than the five defenders on the court.

Concentrating on making shots, especially free throws, was a daunting task as the sounds of the city were everywhere—horns from cars, sirens, and profanity-laced conversations filled the air. Gauging shots against a proper background was a dicey proposition as kids around the court's perimeter ran between parked cars or adults walked back and forth to adjacent grocery stores. Yet, it didn't matter at all. At that time, we played to establish basketball reputations, with neighborhood rivalries and pride at stake. Basketball ruled the city-sports landscape, and there was no need for intruders like the AAU.

That philosophy of the urban youth basketball community was based on maintaining the status quo—"if it ain't broke, don't fix it"—and pride and ownership of basketball as "the city game." The philosophy proved to be shortsighted and stubborn when AAU basketball began to represent progress in the 1980s. As in the Old West, when the railroad replaced the stagecoach, a new day of youth sports in the spring and summer was on the horizon.

Thanks to Nike pitchman and basketball visionary Sonny Vaccaro, AAU started to realize its money-making potential through inner-city basketball and began its well-oiled marketing campaign and expansion. AAU and other youth basketball personnel knew that their newfound Vaccaro-mandated alliance with the sneaker companies was, as

Humphrey Bogart said to Claude Rains in the movie classic *Casablanca*, "the beginning of a beautiful friendship."

AAU, with its long history of accomplishment and know-how in youth sports, had the necessary infrastructure to become the headliner of youth basketball. AAU organized national championships at different age brackets that were the stuff of myth. The best players were reportedly beginning to compete in AAU. And as the bully on the block in this youth basketball explosion, neither the NCAA nor the various state high school federations had very many restrictions or guidelines on what to do about organized spring and summer youth basketball. After all it was the "off season."

It seemed everyone else who would benefit from nationally organized spring and summer basketball saw nothing but open road with all lights flashing green. From college athletic programs and their coaches looking to recruit future stars, to young athletes anxious to participate and play against other cities for pride and scholarship, to parents wanting to provide exposure and the best athletic environment for their children, to dream-selling entrepreneurs sniffing huge profits, Vaccaro's vision was like manna from heaven.

Chapter 5: The Heavyweight vs. Flyweight Bout: Grassroots Basketball in an AAU World

Grassroots coaches with strong principles and good intentions for young athletes face their share of disappointment when entering the often turbulent and muddy waters of AAU and competitive travel basketball. Probably the biggest eye-opening, jaw-dropping disappointment they face is the cutthroat, intense practice of competitors recruiting their players away to other teams or programs.

This fleecing often occurs when players are still in middle school (twelve to fourteen year old age bracket), but they can be even as young as ten years old. Consider this typical recruiting scenario: A well-intentioned coach, new and unsuspecting of the unwritten rules of AAU and competitive travel basketball, enters his team into a tournament supposedly sponsored by AAU. He and his staff have crafted a good team of players from their community. Perhaps the players are friends or teammates of the coach's son, who is also on the team and the primary reason the coach is involved with a basketball program.

The coach is buoyed by the fact that among his collection of athletes is a very talented player with unlimited potential and skills exceeding that of his teammates. He also has a good combination of size and quickness. This player gives the coach confidence that he and the team can compete and possibly win in this initial foray they've made into the unchartered minefield of AAU and competitive travel basketball.

The star player strings together impressive game stats as the team advances through the early rounds of the tournament. He outperforms more highly known prodigies and lo and behold, his team even upsets the sneaker-funded host team of the tournament. This gatecrasher of a squad, led by its exciting head-turning star, strings together more victories during the tournament, exceeding even the expectations of the coach and his staff. AAU euphoria engulfs the entire grassroots organization.

By this point, curious eyes are watching. Texts are sent. Phone camera pictures are snapped. Suddenly more adults are standing around the score table or sitting behind the baskets and along the sideline, watching the young star soar.

As a referee, I have seen this movie before. I talk to the coach before, during, and after the games. The coach speaks enthusiastically about his team, his star player, and his modest goal to have his athletes improve through this venue called AAU basketball, which supposedly provides players exposure and the best competition.

He speaks of his best player, who's in the same grade and school as his son, as a good kid. His family lives just a few blocks away, and the coach knows them well. He expects the team to stay together for the foreseeable future. His thought process is commendable but somewhat innocent. A player this good now has been noticed by sneaker-funded programs, and they are out to corral the best talent to enhance their reputations and profiles, win tournaments, and enlist athletes into their college athletic programs. Their long-term goal is for the athlete to become an NBA player and wear their sneaker for millions of youngsters to see nightly on cable TV.

When the big-picture corporate goals of the deep-pocketed sneaker-funded programs conflict with the altruistic and benevolent goals of the grassroots program, it becomes a heavyweight vs. flyweight battle, intense and often nasty, with preteens caught in the middle.

Chapter 5: The Heavyweight vs. Flyweight Bout: Grassroots Basketball in an AAU World

Suffice to say, when the sneaker-funded programs want a player, they have the resources and knowhow to get him, especially when competing against unwitting grassroots teams. It is generally not even a fair fight.

Oh, the coach of the grassroots program will say this will never happen. The player will be "loyal to me and our program." The coach will speak about providing the player with his start or how he's been a part of our program since church or county youth recreation leagues. The coach may even consider himself the player's guardian. He has provided the youngster with shelter, food, and transportation whenever he encountered problems at home, even before he became interested in basketball. Still, all of this rosy sentiment speaks to an innocence regarding recruiting in competitive travel basketball, an unawareness about the AAU sharks in the water. When the AAU sneaker-funded programs come a-calling, it is just a matter of time before they get their player.

Soon, the young prodigy's family makes a "business" decision, and the player bolts for greener AAU pastures. The idealistic coach faces his toughest loss while learning about this element of competitive youth basketball.

This scenario illustrates how hard it is for grassroots programs to keep their best players. Add to the mix the marketing and trumped-up importance of participating in AAU basketball and the ever-rising entry fees and travel expenses to events alleged to be AAU licensed. Furthermore, as the economy continues to fluctuate, family incomes dip and discretionary spending decreases, the need for an athletic scholarship continues to increase along with the soaring cost of higher education. Taking all this into account, it becomes very easy to see why loyalty almost always loses out to money in today's youth sports culture.

The Sales Pitch

When it's time for well-heeled AAU programs to make a move on an athletic prodigy, they will circumvent his coach and program and reach out to the parents or guardian with a sales pitch on the family sofa. It's a pitch that would make the big time college coach envious as it relates to establishing a connection with the family and highlighting the features and benefits of the "program".

These AAU program adult leaders will discuss and accentuate the success of their programs. They will highlight the parade of local players who, by going through their program, have accepted athletic scholarships to major universities receiving ESPN coverage. Or even better, those players have made it to the NBA. The AAU leaders will emphasize their travel calendar that features trips to exciting venues like Orlando, Las Vegas, and Myrtle Beach, South Carolina. They will boast about how trips to these "showcase" tournaments lead to scholarship offers from the big colleges.

For good measure, these adults will display the gear that separates their program from grassroots one—gleaming silk uniforms with various color combinations and matching pairs of different sneakers. Then there's a final incentive always in the AAU representatives' pocket. They will close the deal by pointing out to the parents that the tab for their athletic prodigy is paid for. There is no membership fee or travel plan or upfront money or monthly payment plan. All of these fees, along with fundraising, are the financial lifeblood of grassroots programs. And just to underscore the point of financial separation between the sneaker-sponsored and grassroots program, the AAU leader will say, "Should you need any assistance at any time, please call."

Chapter 5: The Heavyweight vs. Flyweight Bout: Grassroots Basketball in an AAU World

Manpower and Expertise

Another overlooked aspect of sneaker-sponsored programs is the manpower and expertise they bring to the table when recruiting young athletes. One program that represents these assets is DC Premier, which is more widely known by its former name, DC Assault. Based in metropolitan Washington, DC, DC Assault over the last two decades has been one of the most exalted and prominent AAU basketball programs in the country. The program has sent a litany of players to colleges and universities on athletic scholarships. Many of those athletes, such as former Duke Star Nolan Smith and Kansas State stalwart Michael Beasley and others also played in the NBA.

DC Assault was less like a mom-and-pop youth basketball program and more like a corporation. Under cofounder and leader Curtis Malone, now serving jail time for drug charges and no longer with the organization, the program had time-tested methods for recruiting athletes. In addition, it had an informal organizational chart, official protocols and procedures, a mission statement, a well-deserved reputation of playing a high caliber of tough city basketball featuring highly skilled athletes, and a long track record of success.

DC Assault's reputation and success did not come through happenstance. Malone and his coaches for the various age brackets recruited year round. The organization was very popular in the DC area and well connected and networked in the places where athletes competed, such as recreation centers, CYO gyms, middle schools, and sometimes elementary schools. Public and private school coaches, former and present players, and former and current parents would reach out to Malone or a coach with word of a potential up-and-coming player.

I can remember several instances when, as the referee of a high school game in the cold winter months of January and February, I saw Malone, an Assault assistant coach, or both men together in the lobby of a gym thirty minutes after a game, speaking with a high school coach or player. DC Assault staff would be in the stands, watching players not only at the big games between top ranked city teams, but also at games without high visibility or teams with mediocre records. It didn't matter if the games were in the heart of the city or sometimes thirty miles outside the city in suburbia. Malone and his personnel would be on location and, sure enough, targeting the best player on the court. Whether you were an advocate or detractor of AAU basketball, one had to marvel at the DC Assault corporate model and how Malone and staff conducted business.

The DC Assault hierarchy had an eye for talent. And once their boardroom meetings identified who they wanted, rarely did they fail in landing the player and parents for the program. Their decisions were strictly business based on talent. A hierarchy would place players within team, age and grade classifications based on their skills and, most important, their productivity in the program, similar to a corporation's organization of its staff. Game-by-game evaluations of the players and team-by-team performances in tournaments helped determine the pecking order of players on teams, for instance, the "Gold Team" or "Blue Team," denoting the best and second best teams.(So many players wanted to play for DC Assault that they often had multiple teams in the same age group). This was the youth sports equivalent of department supervisors conducting employee performance reviews.

The corporate reach of DC Assault was extensive. Coaches left the program to take college coaching positions because of their longstanding ties to the program and "inside" connections to talented recruits.

As the standard bearer for AAU and competitive travel basketball, especially in the DC area, DC Assault maintained a company profile and marketing scheme that rivaled McDonald's and Wal-Mart.

Perhaps, the best testimony of the dominant impact of Curtis Malone and DC Assault in the DC area can be traced to the public statements of two prominent basketball coaches at local colleges. In May 2011, the University of Maryland in College Park, located ten minutes north of the city, hired Mark Turgeon, while George Mason University in Fairfax, Virginia, located 30 minutes south of the city, introduced Paul Hewitt as its new head basketball coach. Both men were well respected and successful in the college basketball community, particularly Hewitt with a 2004 Final Four runner-up appearance on his résumé. During their introduction to the sports community, both made it a point to say in media interviews that one of their first priorities was to meet with Malone to establish recruiting ties with the program. The pronouncements by these two esteemed coaches only days apart served as tribute to the depth and reach of Malone and the DC Assault program.

The two-decade dominance of DC Assault is a reminder of how powerful and effective the AAU recruiting machine can be. It's also a reminder of the enormous obstacles that smaller mom-and-pop programs are up against in a climate where the players they seek to develop can be poached at any time by their heavyweight competitors.

Chapter 6: Double Exposure

One of the major selling points for AAU programs, and for competitive travel sports in general, is the opportunity for youth to travel and see different parts of the country. Specifically for athletes in the 9–16 age bracket, traveling means expanding horizons, having new experiences, and pursuing new adventures that produce memories for a lifetime.

Of course the travel experience, at least in AAU and other basketball programs, is largely promoted to mask and counter the criticism that many sporting events are nothing more than money making, overhyped tournaments preying on the egos and obsessions of uninformed parents. The dream-selling businesses in youth sports, with their slick PR professionals, keep the full-court pressure on by highlighting the benefits and virtues of their sporting events so that the parents will not pause and take inventory of the demands put on their family, including the sacrificing of family commitments and vacations. Nor is there mention of the expense breakdowns on these trips that force families to engage in smoke-and-mirrors math as they fail to anticipate all the costs they have to cover.

The marketers of these national tournaments are indeed correct that visiting beautiful and historic places across the country can expose young athletes to many off-the-court opportunities for fun and learning to take place.

But here is the rub: the distance traveled on these trips is a highly overrated perk. Any travel experience—whether you are taking a plane ride across three time zones, renting a tour bus for a 900-mile trip to one of America's most beautiful tourist spots, or just piling athletes in the back of SUVs and

Chapter 6: Double Exposure

Volvos for a 30-minute-long ride outside the city limits—provides opportunities for exposure, fun, growth, and learning off the courts and playing fields.

Three key components, none of which deal with distance traveled, will determine the quality of the experience off the court and fields: the mission of the sports organization, the leadership of the program staff and/or coach, and the selection of the young athletes who participate. These parameters will determine the value of the AAU and competitive travel sport experience as it relates to the education and personal growth of young athletes off the court.

If the sole purpose of a particular organization and coach is to play games, AAU and competitive travel basketball will and can provide it in spades. Local and national tournaments take place virtually every spring & early summer weekend, nearly all promising elite competition, excellent facilities, cost-friendly accommodations, and even college recruiters anxiously awaiting your arrival.

But regardless of the location of the AAU tournament, be it in Orlando or Vegas or just in your neighboring town twenty minutes away, you will end up with only one guarantee: a tight schedule of constant competition, which will take place at high school gyms, recreation centers, or shiny (and not so shiny) sport complexes with upwards of twelve games going on at once. A tournament can include as many as three games a day and possibly a total of five to eight over a three-day weekend, depending on the size of the tournament and the success of your team.

Essentially, if games are the priority of the coach and grassroots youth sports organization, games are what they can find.

Playing Time: Tough Truths about AAU Basketball, Youth Sports, Parents, and Athletes

Ideally, there is a delicate balance between playing a certain number of games and expanding the minds of the young athletes off the court. Uninformed parents more often choose a program for its athletic goals and not its focus on education and development of players as individuals as well as basketball players. The parents generally buy into the program, literally and figuratively, to place their son in an environment where his athletic skills will improve through better competition, and, they hope, he will get more exposure to and eventually interest from colleges (although hoping for interest from colleges for players in this 9-12 age group is nothing more than a pipe dream, with the odds of success similar to those of hitting the state lottery). Nevertheless, even though dream-selling businesses and tournament organizers market tournaments as well-rounded experiences, they leave off-court development up to the grassroots organization.

Accordingly, the organization must make off-court development part of its mission then follow up with a concerted effort to really make it happen. That is why the direction, leadership, and heart of the coach are paramount. However, even with the coach's best intentions to produce an all-around education for the athletes, in most cases, his competitive nature takes over and determines his focus.

The reality is that many coaches in AAU basketball are like the players' parents and are single-minded in the pursuit of their goals. The competitive value of tournaments, not their educational value, is what determines his selection of the travel sites. He has heard word-of-mouth reports of how competitive various tournaments are, how large they are, how much they draw other prominent and top teams from other parts of the country, and how likely it is that top college coaches will be in attendance. Or perhaps, he has been to a tournament previously and knows the competition level is intense. Along with his staff, the coach is concerned with competitive advantages, the other teams in his pool or bracket, opportunities to scout the facilities and other games, travel times to the gymnasiums, and possible practice opportunities between games. In all areas the coach's first priority is to compete and hopefully get notice for his players from college coaches, not the museums, historical landmarks, or the traditional and fine cuisine of the location.

To ensure the team has the best opportunity to win, the coach often places restrictions and curfews on the players, most of which further restrict the sightseeing opportunities to learn about the host city. For example, at tourney sites like Myrtle Beach and Ocean City, Maryland, during down time between games, coaches do not want their players anywhere near the beaches. The coaches know the late-spring and early-summer hot sun can sap players' strength. In fact, the hotel pool will be off limits for the same reason. Likewise, sightseeing tours that require heavy walking are prohibited. Even taking advantage of the fine dining and local delicacies of an area are problematic as a lot of grassroots organizations just don't have the budget for restaurants beyond the buffet-style national chains.

In following his priorities, the coach is right. If his first duty is to win and place his players in the best situation to succeed, he must have rigid measures in place. A good coach should be concerned about "saving the legs" of his players and about ensuring their hydration, nutrition, and proper rest. Yet, it is interesting that at tournaments in the South when indoor gym time is unavailable, some coaches will take the team outside to practice on knee-throbbing asphalt courts, under humid conditions and the glaring sun.

To be fair, some of these decisions are choices coaches have to make based on how the tournament has been set up. With organizers making a three-game guarantee to all teams in a given tournament, there just isn't enough time to accomplish everything. While posted in advance, game times still place time constraints on the team and its leadership. Coaches and leadership must learn travel routes from the hotels and show up to games at least an hour before for procedures like sign-in and the verification of rosters. Proper warm-up and last-minute instruction are always necessary. Generally, games held later in the day are behind schedule and often exceed their allotted slots, and start times get pushed back, perhaps falling thirty minutes or more behind schedule. Consequently the only planning for off—the-court activities deals with getting the players rest and a meal before repeating the agenda for the next day. The scenario generally remains unchanged for the entire weekend.

Perhaps the best and only opportunity to take in the culture and sights of a particular location arises when the team has been eliminated early from advancing in the tournament. Yet most programs simply check out from their hotels and head home. These are mostly working-class folk and must return to work on Monday, so getting an early start on the long drive home becomes the priority.

The Mask

More often than not, grassroots organizations fail to provide that well-rounded off-court experience and education that players need, but sometimes a special coach can make the difference.

One of those coaches is the DC sports icon Edward Hill Jr. Hill, a thunderbolt of energy who stands all of 5 feet, 4 inches and has a fast-talking manner and hearty and easy laugh, is a local sports historian. You would be hard pressed to find someone in DC who knows more about its sports history—particularly its basketball history—than Ed. Just as strong is his ethnic pride, his contributions to his race, and his devotion to youth, especially the young people raised in DC's turbulent quarters.

Professionally, Hill is Howard University's longtime Sports Information Director, and for his tireless work and excellence he was inducted into the Mid-Eastern Athletic Conference (MEAC) Hall of Fame in March 2010. Hill also received the Mary Jo Haverbeck Trailblazer Award, given to pioneers in the sports information profession who have mentored others and helped improve the level of ethnic and gender diversity within the field.

For all his professional achievements and accolades, Hill just as passionately speaks about his twenty-seven years of dedicated voluntary service to youth sports, including twenty-one with youth basketball. It is his heart.

Hill coached the teams of Kingman Pythons AAU during the late 1980s. His teams, mainly comprised of DC youth ages 10–13 from the various Boys and Girls Club recreation centers throughout the city, were generally undersized but also super quick, aggressive, and tenacious. They would press full court the entire game. Proudly representing the DC area, Hill's teams in various age brackets would play in AAU national tournaments held throughout the country, often competing for championships.

Hill's mission was to educate youngsters through basketball and to ensure his players' personal growth and development beyond the game itself. It was a non-negotiable priority for him. He was always concerned about the social development of players and the opportunity for exposure, fun, and learning beyond man-to-man defense and free throw mechanics.

Hill recalls two specific incidents, among hundreds, that only proved that his commitment to his players far exceeded his role as basketball coach.

The first of these occurrences involved one of his eleven-year-old players. Hill was stunned once to find this boy standing on a turbulent DC street corner by himself, waiting for him and the team. Apparently the boy's mom, a single parent, was unable to wait with her son at the appointed place and time when the team was to leave for its ten-day trip to Winter Haven, Florida. Instead, she simply dropped the youngster on the corner with no money or phone and told him to wait until the coach and others arrived.

Hill remembered that later, as each day went by, this quiet, untrusting, and shy youngster became more and more affable. With each new adventure, from eating different foods for the first time to staying with his teammates in a hotel room, laughter and fun became his trademark. He began sporting wide smiles and even wider stares of amazement as the team took in amusement parks, bowling, and miniature golf. Clearly, the young athlete was enjoying life as a carefree youngster. Perhaps, Hill surmised, it was for the first time.

At the conclusion of this particular tournament, as the team boarded the rented minivans for the long trek home, Hill noticed a drastic shift in the player, a complete change from the enthusiastic young lad whose smile shone brighter than the Florida sun. Finally, when the team returned to DC and Hill dropped the player off at his home, it became clear what had transpired during that ride. Upon returning home, the youngster flipped to survival mode to deal with his surroundings. Hill says the boy had put on "the Mask," his strategy for coping and understanding his environment, dealing with adult-type situations, and suppressing his youthful exuberance. Hill felt good about the joy the trip gave the youngster but sad about the price of a lost childhood.

Hill recalls another team trip to Wilmington, North Carolina, when another eleven-year-old player who had never been to a beach shared his fear of the waves. Having spent summers at recreation pools, the young athlete knew how to swim, but this first encounter with the ocean tide intimidated him. Yet over the course of the weeklong stay, he conquered his fear and eventually preferred the shore to the hotel swimming pool. He enjoyed it so much that when it came time for the team to return home, the youngster tried to stay behind by hiding under his hotel-room bed.

Hill admits that his philosophy of total engagement as an AAU coach seemed to place him in the minority of coaches, even at the younger 9–12 age brackets. Hill would cringe when coaches at large tournaments would say to him that they were on a "business trip." Clearly, they had ulterior motives beyond teaching young athletes, and it would show in their demeanor on the court. These coaches berated their players for transgressions, received technical fouls from referees, confronted tournament organizers, and generally acted like the tournament was about them instead of the children.

Hill, by contrast, wanted the full experience for his players. Hill knew that with kids under twelve years old, it's about more than just winning games. Trying to sell the prospect of winning a tournament involving 40 or more teams is virtually setting them up for disappointment. While Hill's teams won tournaments, he also knew that so many things must go right to ever win a national or large tournament.

Hill recognizes the needs of players under 12 years of age. They have, he says, "so much energy, a different energy than teenagers. You have to engage them in other activities off the court. You can't confine them to their hotel quarters between games."

Despite an outstanding track record of on-court success within AAU, Hill left the organization for a competitor, Youth Basketball of America (YBOA). Although clearly not as well-known or competitive as AAU, YBOA nevertheless sponsored national travel tournaments. In keeping with Hill's priorities, the YBOA provided tournament teams a day off from competition. That day off allowed the teams to take in the sights of the city, experience the culture of the locale, learn, and have fun away from the games.

We're at Disney World

Educating young athletes and expanding their horizons and minds can take place without traveling hundreds of miles out of state to a large, highly promoted national tournament. Lessons just as valuable can be taught en route to local competitive basketball events.

Coach Lang Reese can illustrate this point from his own experience. Like his friend and coaching colleague Ed Hill, Reese is a native Washingtonian raised on DC basketball. He also played for renowned St. Anthony High School as well as Hampton University. Reese recalls a valuable lesson when he first took his group of fourteen-year-old DC youth north of the city to a basketball tournament in neighboring Montgomery County, and a heated debate started among the six players in his SUV.

Chapter 6: Double Exposure

As his car crossed the city line, the players became awestruck by the sight of the Washington DC Temple. The beautiful building, constructed in 1968, features six gold spires atop 173,000-square-feet of reinforced concrete covered in Alabama white marble. As the young athletes gawked at the beautiful structure for the first time, a few screamed, "We're at Disney World!" Apparently, they were comparing the temple to the castle they'd watched in television advertisements for Disney World's Magic Kingdom Park.

The players lost all focus and perspective, temporarily forgetting they were headed to play in a basketball tournament. They pleaded with Coach Reese to stop the SUV and take them for a closer look.

Although caught off guard by the Disney World reference, Coach Reese let the conversation continue to see if the players could work out the debate among themselves. That didn't work, and Reese realized he had to provide some clarity for the players. Even after Reese provided the geography lesson and reminded the team that they were outside Washington, DC, and not near Orlando, Florida, the players would not relent. They became more unified in their opinion.

A unique picture had been painted. These teenagers, who had given their trust to Coach to transport them to destinations they never knew before, teach them how to play basketball at a higher level, engage in an endeavor, youth basketball, that they valued most in their lives, and to share with him personal moments that they, perhaps, had not shared with family, had at that moment distrusted his word. Reese saw it all as amusing on some level, as the players were bonding together. Their refusal to accept his knowledge even showed a combativeness that would help them in game competition. Eventually, as the temple receded in the rearview window, the youngsters tempered their enthusiasm, listened, and eventually accepted their coach's word on the Washington, DC Temple. Yet the encounter, at least to Coach Reese, was a learning experience for him just as much as it was for the players.

At that moment, Reese realized just how daunting his task was. He had to educate and expose his players to life and situations beyond basketball and beyond the confines of their immediate neighborhoods. There he was with six teenage black boys about fifteen minutes from their home neighborhoods and five minutes beyond the city limits, and his players had no knowledge about the temple. Reese knew the reality: their confusion was due in part to their neighborhood confinement, as several of the players had never been outside the city. Reese recalled how many of the same players could not tell him which building was the White House or the Capitol when they travelled past both earlier in the season.

Nevertheless, this moment was different. The player's intensity and stubborn assurance that they were at Disney World spoke of their lack of exposure. And it posed a range of challenges that made carrying out his mission even more intimidating going forward.

Of equal concern was how easily the Disney World debate totally distracted the players. Reese, while acknowledging the short attention span of young teens, was still concerned about how quickly the players' attention could be diverted, even from playing basketball. It bothered Reese because he knew how fast things happen in their neighborhoods, even within their homes and families. He saw this incident as a wake-up call, revealing just how much work he had to do, teaching his players self-discipline, focus, sacrifice, and determination both on and off the court.

Chapter 6: Double Exposure

Five years later, Reese would come to say that what he learned from the young players was just as important as what he hoped he had taught them. Coach would value moments to teach and educate the players. The opportunity to talk and discuss their daily issues was, to him, of equal and perhaps far greater value than the outcome of games played in one of so many faceless weekend tournaments.

Reese encouraged his players to express their thoughts, to ask questions without restraint or embarrassment. The youngsters, so street-savvy and instinctive and yet so unenlightened in many other ways, made for unique and rewarding journey companions, with hoops as the common path for Reese and his players.

Chapter 7: Coach, If You Cut Me I'll Murder You

As the previous chapters have shown, there are many impostors who claim to represent grassroots basketball and the strong principles it imparts to young players. In the world of youth sports, there are countless unsung men and women who define grassroots basketball in the truest sense of the word. This chapter and the next share inspiring stories of Lang Reese, a coach who is dedicated to meaningfully touching the lives of his players. When basketball programs like his combine patience and selflessness with egoless and committed leadership, they paint a portrait of youth sports at its best.

***

DeWayne Franklin was a physically menacing man-child. At sixteen he was 6 feet, 5 inches and 250 pounds before breakfast. The teenager's size, dark complexion and dreadlocks could make a stranger uneasy. Quite aware of his intimidating presence, DeWayne moved about freely without the repercussions that others might find walking alone on the turbulent streets of urban Washington, DC. To make matters dicier, DeWayne had a quick wit, acerbic tongue, defiant attitude, and short attention span. His hardcore upbringing at the infamous Sursom Corda projects in the center of the city exposed him to many things most adults don't see in a lifetime.

Consequently, DeWayne could alarm others with his stature as well as with his words and imagination. When those elements combined with his mischievous, attention-seeking nature, he could be quite a handful.

DeWayne excelled in the DC art of "jonin," an activity typically called "playing the dozens" in other places. Suffice to say, if DeWayne had you in his crosshairs, you had best have thick skin and a quick comeback. Otherwise you'd be in

71

for a long slew of insults and barbs you could do nothing about. You knew you couldn't win if you chose to fight him.

As with most big kids, DeWayne was encouraged to play ball. His game of choice was basketball, and he displayed some talent. He could put the ball on the floor and actually beat you off the dribble to the basket, or he could hit a little pull-up jumper. His jump shot was serviceable from up to fifteen feet from the basket.

This was indeed a bonus as generally most "bigs" from the city playgrounds, or even those fortunate enough to play in a Boys Club or AAU program, were recruited to stay under the basket, defend, and rebound. Often in youth basketball, big kids are not trained or required to do much else. This is because most youth league and even high school coaches don't have the time or patience, or sadly the know-how (or even sadder the inclination), to learn to teach big-man fundamentals. Furthermore, most coaches generally were never "bigs" but instead were guards and forwards with a natural penchant toward teaching perimeter skills. Thus "bigs" like DeWayne, while always sought after as assets for winning, are sent packing to basketball's low post for a steady diet of hitting the boards and defending.

DeWayne, on the other hand, enforced his will physically and verbally to get the ball from teammates and do with it what he wanted. Often when he got a defensive rebound, DeWayne would take the ball the length of the court to shoot, ignoring his teammates. Not too many teammates wanted to openly challenge him.

Coach Lang Reese was raised on DC basketball. As a talented player in the early '70s, he played at renowned basketball power St. Anthony High School just after legendary Coach John Thompson had left the small Catholic school and headed to a Hall of Fame career across town at Georgetown University.

After playing basketball and graduating from Hampton University, Reese stayed an avid fan of basketball and especially DC basketball —though from a distance. Like most former players, he took exceptional pride in the DC brand of ball at all levels, from professional to scholastic. Like most former players, he had strong opinions on who could and couldn't play, who could and couldn't coach. And like most former players, this was the length of his reach—go to games, stay abreast of the latest hoops' comings and goings, and sit back and reminisce about how ball back in the day was clearly better compared to the hoops played today.

One day a friend, tired of hearing him bemoan city ball and the negative impact it had on city youth, challenged Reese to get involved. Rising to the challenge, Reese decided to enter the subculture of youth basketball, specifically AAU, and become a coach.

A successful businessman, Reese did not enter this arena haphazardly. He networked, consulted, and watched how AAU and the competitive travel basketball business was conducted. He mapped out his strategy for recruiting athletes and, more importantly, getting both physical and emotional support from parents and coaching staff. He sought financial support through corporate and small business contributions.

Finally, into the fray he leaped. His first teams were thirteen-year-old suburban kids from neighboring counties outside DC. The teams were short on size, short on roster numbers, and short on talent—all attributes typical of a start-up grassroots program. But he had parental buy-in and transportation to get the players to practice, games, and tournaments. And while consultations with veteran coaches informed him he was dutifully following the AAU way, the experience nonetheless left Reese empty inside.

He wanted to make a bigger impact. He wanted to provide opportunities to the often neglected city players to enhance their games and expand their options, explore new adventures, and basically flourish like the suburban kids who generally had resources, money, and two-parent households.

After one summer AAU tournament, I was with Reese when we stood in front of Archbishop McNamara High School in Forestville, Maryland, just outside the city in predominantly black Prince George's County, and spoke with three prominent black men who were successful leaders of suburban AAU programs. Reese told them of his plans to go into the city and recruit players.

In unison, reminiscent of a Baptist church choir and with pained expressions as if just finding that their BMWs had been stolen from the parking lot, the trio pleaded with Reese not to go into the city. They warned him that the city kids come with too much baggage—bad attitudes, bad habits, lack of commitment, and poor discipline. The kids and their scholastic coaches would never be loyal, there would be no parental support, and the ultimate deal breaker, the parents would not pay!

These "three wise men," these hypocrites, had built their successful programs under the guise of providing opportunities for young, predominantly black athletes. It's true, they did provide this service on some level, but their first loyalty was to their own budding dream-selling businesses and fat wallets. The way they trivialized Reese's idea clearly illustrated this point. How could it be anything else when they were so cavalier and dismissive? They saw no value in thirteen-year-old black boys from the city. The sad irony is that the neighborhood drug dealers find great value in those same boys.

Reese, a product of the same DC neighborhoods, knew after that conversation that he was obligated to get his players from the streets of DC.

Three years later, the three wise men, hypocrites all, were indeed prophetic. Every problem they listed clanged true and loud like coins from a casino slot machine cascading into the winner's bucket. In fact, Reese encountered even more problems than the three wise men predicted on that summer evening. Getting players, however, was never a problem. Athletes were always available and anxious to play. After all, they had heard about AAU and wanted the same opportunities to play but were always beaten down by the excuses adults make to cover up their own apathy. Since the excuses all run together like so many other roadblocks and obstacles in city life, the youngsters just accept rejection and defeat as normal, giving credence to the low expectations and reasons for them not to try, not to dream.

Meanwhile Reese, now seeing the problems firsthand, formed an even stronger resolve to give DC youngsters a chance. In truth, Reese had, like many folks, only a cursory knowledge of what was going on with our youth. He was really caught off guard by the depth, range, and multitude of the problems he faced. Raised in DC and still a resident there, he understood how positive and life altering a relationship with sports can be—specifically basketball, the city's game. It impassioned and motivated him to press forward with his mission. But now he was finding out the difference between thinking you know the problems and solutions—after all, he was a product of the same environment—to being on the front line and taking ownership of the problems and solutions.

Reese found out very quickly that the process of trying to give youngsters a chance to better themselves through basketball did not form a straight-line path. It wasn't a simple good vs. bad, connect-the-dots situation. His efforts, indeed his mission to provide opportunities through spring and summer youth basketball, were met with distrust and skepticism. But Reese was fortified by the battle cry of "Don't recruit those city kids!" He knew turning back was not an option. He was in for the long haul.

One thing he knew to be consistently true: the ballplayers in the city were fearless and played hard. Almost in spite or perhaps because of their environment, they played the game with a single-minded pride and resolve, as if they were saying, "This game, right now, I can manage. Maybe things off the court are unsettled and problematic, but on this court I'm in control." Coach Reese knew this intensity could overcome many shortcomings such as lack of exposure to the game or a lack of fundamentals, talent, or size. He would teach and work through these issues. But the players had to be willing to compete and fight. Reese would often say, "You can't win with all choir boys." He sought city kids with an edge to them.

As Coach Reese's program became better established and known throughout AAU circles, many of the public high school coaches in DC became eager to work with him and have their athletes play in his AAU program. Generally, AAU recruiting is a slippery slope because high school coaches, especially public school staffs, do not trust AAU folk. They are rightfully fearful that these AAU programs will "steal" their athletes and encourage them to transfer to more visible and attractive programs with shiny new gyms, well-stocked weight rooms, a winning tradition, and a schedule of thirty-five games or more. Some private schools are always on the prowl for hidden talent; through their business relationships, they have been known to compensate AAU coaches to recruit new talent. Coach Reese distinguished himself from the AAU pack with a recruiting pitch to the public school coaches that entailed two simple statements: "I will return your player to you at the end of the AAU season." And, "I work for nobody and just want to provide an opportunity for the athlete."

Eventually skepticism gave way to enthusiasm, and as Coach Reese's winning program moved up to the higher age brackets, coaches called him to provide player recommendations. Coaches such as Bill Wilkerson at H.D. Woodson, Bill Truehart at Paul Laurence Dunbar, Rob Nickens at Theodore Roosevelt, and Vaughn Jones at Calvin Coolidge were always generous with players and, when Coach needed it, access to their gyms for practices—a huge asset for resource-poor grassroots programs. Still, I was Coach Reese's main referral source for players. As a referee working the city public high school games, and as a high school teammate and good friend, I supported his mission to help city athletes. I identified players I had refereed and thought he needed to see for his program. I also knew he wanted players with an "edge."

On one occasion I recommended that Coach come see a hard-playing, gritty yet skilled player from Spingarn High in northeast DC. I had spoken to the young man after officiating two of his games, and he was eager to play AAU basketball at the end of the high school season. Reese was anxious to attend a game and make the necessary sales pitch to Keith Jackson, the player's coach and a former standout player from the city. Jackson had played college ball at Old Dominion University before becoming a head coach at Spingarn.

However, the very next morning following my glowing reviews of the player, the *Washington Post* headlines shared that the youngster had been arrested for killing another teenager at a 7-Eleven three weeks earlier. Immediately, I get a call from Reese with his stipulation: "Kev, I want kids with an edge, but this is *over the edge.*"

Having refined our understanding of that desired edge in a player, Reese recruited DeWayne Franklin. Not only was Franklin big—an attractive trait in its own right—he was physical, nasty, and petulant on the court. DeWayne was not highly recruited to play since he had raw skills and played at a DC public school without much fanfare and exposure. Of course, he perpetuated the stereotypes of DC kids that the three wise men promoted. DeWayne was, however, an easy "get" for Reese's program. Indeed, he fit the profile that Coach thrived on—a tough hombre needing a chance to play and thankful for the opportunity. He also epitomized the three wise men's warning about city players.

DeWayne was a force to be reckoned with off the court. To call his home life unsettled is to call a hurricane a summer breeze. Often, instead of staying at his house he stayed with his older brother and girlfriend, sleeping on their floor. At school he was a handful and then some. While a capable student, he preferred to instigate and "jone" than study, which often led to fights and suspensions. School administrators, realizing the ineffectiveness of home suspensions, instead gave DeWayne in-school suspensions, which consisted of him spending the bulk of the day in a classroom by himself. Eventually, Reese was listed as DeWayne's emergency contact—a hat Coach would wear for several of his players. There seemed to be plenty contacts for an emergency involving DeWayne. However, Coach could talk sense to him. He would tell him, "I don't want to hear what happened. I'm telling you what is going to happen from this point forward."

DeWayne respected the not-buying-your-nonsense, looking-you-straight-in-the-eye manner of Coach, especially when the punishment for misconduct meant missing games, tournaments, and even practice.

Still the relationship with DeWayne was a give-and-take affair that both rewarded Coach and gave him headaches. DeWayne, truth be told, immensely enjoyed the AAU experience more than he would let on to the other players, perhaps more than he would admit to himself. Young folk in the rough quarters of the city don't hang too tightly to "things" like housing, family, school, and friends. Life is subject to constant change, and those things are often sources of disappointment. So to guard against pain and rejection, young people like DeWayne wear the protective armor of nonchalance and maintain a take-it-or-leave-it attitude that says, "This doesn't mean anything to me anyway."

Yet, Reese knew otherwise.

DeWayne would call to confirm game dates, even practice dates. Always needing a ride to and from gym sites, he would call Coach with anxiety in his voice if Coach was running late. "Coach, where you at? You still coming to get me? You lost?" DeWayne would pester Coach in rapid fire without waiting for a reply. Words would not pacify DeWayne. Lessons of the street taught him to trust only what he could see, and until he saw Coach's Chevy Tahoe SUV, DeWayne could not find peace.

Once in the car and feeling secure and included, DeWayne would start in on the other players. "Coach, why you bring these guards? They can't play," he would call out. "We need to get some better guards." Looking at teammate and shooting guard Darryl Waller, DeWayne would say, "You got crushed last game. You can't play. You gonna be a sandwich artist at Subway." DeWayne would carry on like the host of his own sports talk radio show the entire trip. Most of the players laughed; others fired back to no avail or turned up the car radio or adjusted their headphones. Even Coach's order to shut up only bought a five to ten minute grace period before DeWayne was at it again.

DeWayne was enjoying himself, and Reese knew it despite the headaches. When the team prepared to take trips to places like Philadelphia, Richmond, and North Carolina, and eventually Florida and Las Vegas, DeWayne could hardly contain his enthusiasm and would bombard Reese with phone calls. Eventually he would force himself to ignore DeWayne's worrisome requests to rehash the same itinerary. On trips, DeWayne noted the simplest things, like having clean sheets on the bed in the hotel. Or how quiet and dark it was at night.

Chapter 7: Coach, If You Cut Me I'll Murder You

On the court, DeWayne played a team game. He listened to Reese. He didn't complain about minutes. He passed the ball on offense. On defense he relished the role of enforcer. Although not the tallest or longest player on the 17 & Under team—by then Reese had recruited five players 6 feet, 8 inches or taller—DeWayne was still the meanest and fiercest, and definitely the most fearless. Consequently, DeWayne felt a sense of responsibility. He saw himself as the only player in this role and thus took ownership as "big brother." While the other "bigs" had more skills, he was the defensive stopper, which gave him a defined role. Again, he felt secure and included.

DeWayne, as the enforcer, would help lead the team to victories. When DeWayne would enter the game, you could see a change take place. Not only was his physical stature imposing, but his physicality impacted games. Opposing guards would shy away from uninhibited forays down the lane, and entry passes into the post were less frequent as the opposition "bigs" didn't quite post up as strong or even want the ball with the same vigor as they had earlier in the game.

It seemed the "DeWayne Franklin Threat" was especially effective against suburban teams and smaller city teams that were intimidated by the overall size of Reese's teams, the physical presence of DeWayne, and the fact that the team was from Washington, DC. Teams often would psyche themselves out. If the games became overly physical, DeWayne was the first on the scene with a glint in his eye that said he was very comfortable with taking matters to another level, within or outside the rules. Usually, opponents shyly returned their focus to basketball, but a valuable message about "established territory" had been sent.

Coach admired DeWayne's fearlessness. Truth be told, it was what made DeWayne one of Reese's favorite players. While Reese maintained his commitment to providing opportunities for young inner city players like DeWayne, nevertheless, he remained a competitor at heart and wanted to win. Knowing that his roster would not have many, if any, of the so-called top talented players in the area, he knew that his players would have to compete harder and literally outfight the competition, often winning on toughness. This strategy, with DeWayne as the spark plug, worked well. As Reese's teams moved to the older AAU age brackets—15 & Under, 16 & Under, and 17 & Under—they would win or have high finishes in local tournaments. In fact, under the team name of Blackhawks, his teams would exact revenge on teams that had earlier in the younger age brackets spanked his players.

Revenge was especially sweet when Reese conquered the teams coached by the three wise men who had warned him against recruiting city players like DeWayne. When Reese expanded his schedule to compete in Nike or Adidas sneaker-sponsored tournaments in Myrtle Beach (South Carolina), Richmond (Virginia), Orlando (Florida), and eventually Las Vegas, his teams won their share of games, upsetting nationally recognized programs that featured D-I recruits heading to frontline college programs. At one national tournament in Hampton, VA, the Blackhawks were the only non-sponsored team to advance out of pool play in the over eighty team Nike sponsored event.

Coach cited two primary factors for the success of his teams: 1) an inner toughness and tenacity, and 2) a chip-on-the-shoulder, inner-city warrior mentality that showed they could play against anybody. His teams dispensed intimidation as opposed to being intimidated. Quite frankly, many of the teams and players they played were over-hyped by the media machines, including the so-called experts with their scouting and tout-sheet player rankings listed in their publications and blogs. Player evaluation is an inexact science, and many of these scouting services compile and get their data in many different and conflicting ways.

During his entire AAU and competitive travel basketball coaching career, Coach never had a player who achieved first-team All-City or All-County status in high school. Indeed, his program was a collection of players who just wanted an opportunity to play. His best player was Maurice (Moe) Pearson. A 6-foot, 5-inch thirteen-year-old, Pearson had been cut by one of the marquee AAU programs in the area. Coach signed him up. As Pearson grew to 6-feet, 9-inches and developed his skills under Coach's watchful tutelage, Pearson became a player that other programs coveted and attempted to steal. However, always appreciative for the second chance from Coach, Pearson and his mom never considered leaving the program. Pearson played for Coach for four AAU and competitive travel basketball seasons. Realizing that Pearson was just as talented as many of the athletes he played against in the AAU and competitive travel basketball circuit, and wanting him to get maximum exposure and interest from colleges, Coach called one of the touting/recruiting services to promote the player. Instantly a recruiter became interested in the efforts of the 6-foot, 9-inch player who competed in the renowned basketball hotbed of Washington, DC, and who played on a winning AAU program and high school team (Pearson's Bethesda-Chevy Chase high school team finished runner-up in the MD 4A State tournament his senior season). A scoop like this—finding a blue chip prospect—would provide the recruiter a major leg up on the competition. The following conversation occurred:

Recruiter: Can the kid really play?

Coach Reese: No doubt! He's my best player and led us in rebounds and points. (He highlighted tournaments in which Pearson played well and outshone more highly rated players.)

Recruiter: (Clearly excited) Where do *you* want me to rank him (as a rising senior for the upcoming season)? Top 50? Top 25?

Coach Reese: (Caught off guard by such an offer sight unseen by the recruiter) Oh, I'm not sure. But Top 75 will be fine.

Recruiter: No problem.

Whether the exposure that Coach provided helped or not, Moe Pearson signed with Ohio University. After transferring to NAIA powerhouse Georgetown (KY), Pearson starred for the school, graduated, and today is playing professionally in Belgium.

Maurice Pearson and DeWayne played the backline of defense for Coach's team. After the Blackhawks added another three or four players over 6-feet, 8-inches, including shot-blocking seven-footer Justin Frank, opposing teams struggled to score. Yet all was not well. DeWayne remained a headache off the court. His relentless jonin and hyperactivity frustrated many of his teammates.

An AAU team roster is constantly changing—if not from game to game or tournament to tournament, then surely from season to season. So the ties that bind a local high school team, such as shared classes, same teachers, and same neighborhood, do not apply to AAU teams. Establishing unity is thus a precarious venture. Often players don't even try out or compete to make a team. They are selected by referral or teammate connection or favor from a multitude of sources— friends, family, coach (high school, prospective college). The players are, in essence, given a spot on the team without working for it. This, in turn, occasionally fosters in players an inflated ego and sense of entitlement. Of course, their parents share that same ego and entitlement, which often proves to be even more troublesome.

It is hard to blame athletes from getting big egos. Most AAU programs have a cursory tryout process. It is more or less a quick money grab for the programs as athletes are charged a fee ($10–$25 or more) for a two- or three-day tryout to compete for few open roster spots. Once these positions are filled and practices and games follow, subsequent player additions usually occur by word of mouth. Thus, the athlete and parent joining the team often adopt a new-sheriff-in-town attitude that destroys team chemistry and sets the stage for a me-first mindset.

Reese knew about this issue. And while he often took youngsters by referral, it wasn't merely because the young man could bring wins. It was generally out of a team need to enhance the team's play while providing another young man an opportunity. With his grassroots city program, Reese was not adding blue chippers headed to Duke or Georgetown. Consequently, he would not tolerate ego-tripping athletes nor whining, demanding, and noncompliant parents.

To keep this goal intact, Coach Reese wielded a big hammer as enforcement: the power to cut a player swiftly. From his conversation with the three wise men, Reese learned it was best to fund his own program. This was effective not only because kids from DC probably could not contribute financially, but more importantly, when parents pay for programs they often feel they have a decision making voice equal to "management" (i.e., the coach).

Reese was having none of that. By keeping fee requests to just the bare essentials—registration costs and meal money on road trips (which rarely happened)—he had the management system he wanted: a dictatorship. He could tell a parent to "take your child and find another program" in a minute. During the early years of Reese's program and in the younger age groups, player turnover was more an outcome of parents' decisions than the attitudes of the players.

Reese's strong vision and organizational framework were in place. His team had a half-dozen players who had been with the program for four years. The only problem was DeWayne, who was on the verge of uprooting everything Reese had systematically put in place.

DeWayne had the respect of his teammates on the court, but there were times when they did not fully grasp his contributions, subtle basketball nuances such as a "box out" or "screen for a teammate" or "off-the-ball defense," which were only appreciated by a coaching staff. These nuances definitely weren't appreciated by parents. Off the court, DeWayne's constant and seemingly nonstop mockery alienated players. Nobody wanted to room with him on the road because he would talk or watch TV all night long. In practice he would badger and pick on players. He was a handful, and none of the players wanted to deal with him. Reese would prevent, control, mediate, discipline, and squash issues each time they arose, but like an ever-rolling tide, another issue would flair up. Getting frustrated, at times Reese would tell DeWayne he was going to have to cut him or suspend him from the team if he didn't settle down.

Reese didn't want to take this action and he never gave it serious thought. In fact, he thought the other players needed to toughen up and not be so thin-skinned. Nevertheless, he spoke to DeWayne and told him he had better not fight one of the players. But this was not a huge concern. DeWayne was not a bully but more of a beehive nuisance. If anything, DeWayne was just trying to maximize the enjoyment of the moment, the same as we would getting together with high school teammates or classmates after a long absence.

On the other hand, Reese also knew that good AAU and competitive travel teams need team unity and chemistry—a key element to winning. It happens through bonding on road trips, sharing battles and close games in hostile away gyms, eating buffet meals at discount fast food restaurants, and enduring crammed long car rides and four-players-to-a-room motel stays. So Reese knew that a balancing act was necessary to give DeWayne the opportunity to better himself and provide a rewarding experience for the other players.

The players and the parents, however, lost patience and didn't understand. They had had enough. The parents met among themselves and decided to approach Reese, requesting that DeWayne be removed from the team. Reese and his assistant coach, Clarence Claiborne, whose son Clarence Jr. was among the program's first recruits, were the only adults who didn't want DeWayne out. Reese even had doubts about Claiborne, as his son had many a shouting match with DeWayne on and off the court. But to his credit, Claiborne did not side with the parents in the meeting.

Reese gave the parents a forum and listened. He did not have to. To the credit of the parents, their complaint took the form of a request and not a directive. Reese probably would have told them to take their children and go if they had approached him in any other manner. He knew what he had done for their athletes in terms of providing exposure to college recruiters and, for that matter, exposure to different life experiences. He knew they had improved as basketball players. And he knew the parents recognized the growth that had taken place. He had met, to the letter, his mission statement for the program. DeWayne would stay on the team until he decided otherwise.

The possibility of "otherwise" came soon after that meeting. DeWayne got into a fight with another player.

Jordan Johnston, a 6-foot, 5-inch, 230-pound forward, had been added to the team via a referral from a college coach whom Reese respected as having an eye for talent. As promised, the athlete had some talent, but he was also lazy and unmotivated, perhaps explaining why he had already attended three high schools. He was quiet and didn't really click with the other team players in general. Taking into account Jordan's loner nature, in total opposition to DeWayne's personality, and marginal contributions to helping this particular team win, most could have predicted an altercation would take place.

DeWayne didn't regard Jordan as a teammate but more of an interloper. He didn't respect his game. DeWayne and many of his teammates felt Jordan shot the ball too much without doing other things like rebounding and defending. Off the court, DeWayne noticed the gulf between Jordan and the rest of the team. Consequently, DeWayne's big brother instincts took over and a scuffle ensued. To make matters worse, this happened not at a practice but at a hotel on a road trip.

Reese was incensed.

Upon returning home from the trip, Reese purposely dropped everybody off first, leaving just him and DeWayne in the car. Reese had told DeWayne repeatedly both in private and in front of the team that he was going to "cut him" or "suspend him from an out of town trip" if he didn't straighten up. It would work for a moment and DeWayne would shape up, albeit briefly. Mostly it was a wink-wink way of getting DeWayne's attention—the same as a coach loudly blowing his whistle in practice.

However, this time DeWayne knew he was in trouble. Reese, after speaking in general about the trip and the team, told DeWayne about the seriousness of his error. But cutting DeWayne was never going to be an option. This was a serious discussion about more than basketball. Posturing and idle threats were off the table. This was about mentoring, which to Reese was more important than any AAU game and a part of his program's mission.

As the conversation progressed, DeWayne became more and more fidgety. Finally, assuming that getting cut was where the conversation was going, DeWayne exclaimed, "Coach, if you cut me I'll murder you!"

Now, this wasn't the first time Reese had heard DeWayne say something like this. In the car with teammates he would whisper threats about Coach to the other players loud enough so that he could hear. For effect, DeWayne would also repeat how he would "torch Coach's car" or other fake acts of machismo to strengthen his image in front of the other players. Reese knew this was nothing more than tough guy posturing and never gave it serious thought. In fact, Reese attributed mere symbolism to the words DeWayne used. He felt DeWayne and his choice of words epitomized the need for his program and the reason he started the venture to help city young men in the first place. It reaffirmed his mission statement to expose young men in the city to another way, a different way of life, an alternative lifestyle, a choice—all provided with basketball as the hook.

Reese realized that DeWayne's use of the word *murder* spoke volumes about his background. DeWayne said "murder," but if most young people had the courage to jone on the coach in the first place, they would have used the word "kill." It is acceptable and used frequently by coaches and players in sports language and has several meanings. In sports parlance it is very prevalent. "He's getting killed out there" refers to a situation where a player is being dominated by an opponent.

Using the word *murder* has no other meaning. It's not a slang term or code word. It stands alone as a vicious act. When

DeWayne used the word, it spoke to his background. It spoke to his environment. It spoke to what he had been exposed to in his brief sixteen years of life. It spoke to his day-to-day existence.

Yet, as DeWayne used the phrase again that night as the two drove home, it provided a new meaning to Reese, one that he never saw coming. He saw caring, possessiveness, ownership, and purpose, as DeWayne was really saying how much the coach and team meant to him in the only way a towering, glowering gladiator from the mean streets knew how to express himself. DeWayne's words were never a threat, but a cry. Only his background didn't allow for displays of weakness, pleas for forgiveness, or requests for second chances.

Even now, with possibly his basketball future at stake, with the single most important thing that had provided him joy and attention for the last couple of springs and summers in jeopardy, even now, in front of one of the few adults he most admired and respected, DeWayne still hid behind the mask of inner city toughness. Yet Coach knew that DeWayne was admitting how deeply he cared about being a part of Reese's program. AAU basketball and Coach Reese gave DeWayne inclusion and security in an otherwise tumultuous life.

Reese continued the conversation as if the words were never spoken. Coach was never intent on breaking DeWayne down, but on using the conversation as a teachable opportunity for growth and development.

It was a watershed moment for DeWayne. He was finally beginning to grasp accountability, discipline, and big-picture consequences, a very hard sell for many tough young men like DeWayne who rely on instincts from day to day. DeWayne remained on the team.

Ultimately, DeWayne's playful demeanor did not change. He still needed to be packaged as "flammable," but he was evolving, he was growing up. To Coach Reese, this was a victory greater than any posted on a gymnasium scoreboard.

Moreover, Reese found the face of his program. He knew what sports could do, but probably never thought it would manifest itself as clearly as it did with DeWayne. Indeed, most coaches in AAU programs tend to measure their success in the number of players that play ball on the next levels of high school or college. But teaching critical thinking and patience in decision-making to a young man like DeWayne, while the impact is harder to gauge, is the best success story.

Reese would have over forty young men in his program over the six years he ran an AAU basketball program. He helped most players in ways far greater than in the teaching of drop-step moves and free-throw mechanics. He helped by deed, by actions, with mentoring, discipline, and caring, and by being an example of a positive black male leader.

Through many of the same contacts he used to recruit players for his AAU program, Coach Reese was able to get a workout for DeWayne with John Wiley, then head coach at Prince George's Community College in Largo, Maryland, located fifteen minutes outside DC. After graduating from high school, DeWayne Franklin attended the college and played basketball for Coach Wiley and the Owls.

Chapter 8: A Honey Bun and Cream Soda

I marvel at young black athletes from the most impoverished neighborhoods. For many of these athletes, what happens on the court is the easiest part of their day. Many coaches, white and black, and including those aforementioned three wise men, lament how city ballers are undisciplined, issue-laden, high-maintenance problem children.

And to them I say, what's your point?

Do you only want to coach a pristine, yes-sir, no-sir, dutiful, comfortable, college-bound son or daughter with both parents at home and a two-car garage?

If so, your opportunities are plentiful in the Washington, DC, area. The surrounding suburban communities—Fairfax County, Virginia, and Montgomery County, Maryland—are listed as two of the wealthiest counties in the nation. You really won't have to travel far beyond the city limits to coach teams comprised mostly of players with spotless backgrounds. Many of the private schools located in Washington, DC, have excellent academic programs with yearly tuitions rivaling or exceeding those of many colleges and universities. The students are among the country's elite, including the children of US presidents past and present. They have first rate facilities, marvelous sports programs, admirable community involvement and parental support, and competent and deep coaching staffs.

A head coach at one of these schools can establish a legacy of winning ballgames and conference championships, yet never touch a youngster's soul or inspire or challenge a player beyond sharing with him or her the scouting report and game plan for an opponent.

Chapter 8: A Honey Bun and Cream Soda

What is most unsettling is the observation that these are "nice and good kids." I'm sure they are. But is that "nice and good kids" assessment freestanding or made in comparison to young people from less fortunate environments like those from the inner city?

My keenness and chip-on-the-shoulder racial pride force me to pose the question in even the most docile of environments.

I was attending a football game at Maret High School, a private school with a tuition north of $30,000 and located in upper northwest DC. Someone driving by the gated school with circular driveways could easily miss it, even with the aid of GPS, as it easily blends in with the old-money community of multi-million dollar homes and international embassies it shares along magnificent tree-lined streets.

At the conclusion of a fall afternoon high school football game, standing on the field as the Maret players headed to the locker room, I along with a couple of fathers slapped hands in congratulations with the players. All the players were respectful, polite, looked you in the eye, and said "thank you." Indeed they seemed like nice young men, and I instantly felt good about their bright futures. One of the parents said they were "nice and good kids," surely without any intent or agenda. I agreed with him.

But I could not let the comment stand alone. Instantly I said, "They should be! I bet 90 percent of the players come from upper-middle-class households with two parents. In certain parts of the city, I could show you where perhaps only 10 percent of the young people have two-parent households." Clearly, this wasn't the forum for this discussion, judging from the awkward silence and the "what's with you" wide-eyed stares I received. And probably the fathers—two black and two white—were right in what they were nonverbally communicating.

When I hear "nice and good kids," which happens far more frequently in the suburbs than in the city, instantaneously I get defensive. Its reflexive and a matter of pride. I want who said it, black or white, to know that affluence doesn't give children a monopoly on being "nice and good."

Many black youngsters in challenging environments are just as good, just as nice, and just as smart, and perhaps more resourceful.

I want "nice and good" to be replaced with "well supported." The difference between these players at Maret School and some youth in rough neighborhoods across town that have too much going on is that the Maret players are well supported by a network of attentive adults, a strong infrastructure, exposure to positive experiences, the challenge of high expectations, and the best facilities, equipment, and training.

Many city ballplayers go without so often that we cavalierly dismiss the impact of their day-to-day struggles and hardships. I cringe as if listening to nails on the chalkboard when I hear coaches whine about city players. That young players endure so many detour-filled and chaotic daily struggles, often not of their own making, elicits my respect for their determination to compete in sports at such a high and accomplished level.

***

Fourteen-year-old Darryl Waller was one of Coach Lang Reese's first city recruits. Excelling in football and basketball, his athletic skills were superior to other athletes his age. He moved with a grace and smoothness that gave the impression he was just coasting. Adults and coaches, on the other hand, instantly compared him to an untamed colt, still growing into his untapped talent with stardom in his future. Adults marveled at his sudden stop-and-go, his explosions to the basket, his speed up and down the floor, and especially his court awareness that belied his fourteen years.

Even exceeding his physical gifts was his personality— on and off the court. A megawatt smile was always apparent. He playfully, with a butterfly-like easiness, bounced in and out from brief conversation to brief conversation, always exiting with a smile. He spoke with self-confidence, displaying none of the reticence and distrust around strangers, especially adults, usually associated with tough city youth. In fact, considering his talent and potential, he was probably too comfortable and at ease with adult strangers. Surely, with his burgeoning talents, coaches and others would be on the prowl to do whatever was necessary to get Darryl on a roster.

In truth, I guess I fit that bill as an individual on the youth talent prowl. At the time, I was the referee in a neighborhood police-organized tournament at Boys and Girls Club #10 on 14th Street in northwest DC. A five-minute ride from Howard University, it was a community not to be played with. After one of the games, I approached Darryl about playing AAU with Coach Reese. Without hesitation Darryl gave me his full name and phone number. It struck me that this was too easy. In fact, if any exchange of information was to take place, it should have been me giving him Coach Reese's number. Perhaps because I had refereed the two games Darryl had played that day and we had had a brief dialog, he felt some sort of hoops connection and had given me street credentials.

When Coach Reese reached Darryl at the phone number he provided, he learned Darryl was anxious to play and wanted to attend a practice to get started. Yet, it would be six months before Coach Reese would actually meet with Darryl. Subsequent phone calls went unreturned and eventually the number was no longer valid. Only through a chance meeting between tournament organizer Ed Hill and Darryl were Coach Reese and Darryl able to reconnect.

It wasn't that Darryl didn't want to play. City life for youngsters like Darryl moves fast, lacks order and structure, and forces young boys to often make adult decisions that they are not equipped to process. Apparently, Darryl had broken a bone in his arm playing football and therefore decided playing basketball that season wasn't an option so, again, wearing the city armor of indifference and low expectations, he simply moved on. He had essentially quit playing AAU before he got started, while seeing no value in himself past his talent to play ball.

Only this time Darryl Waller decided to call coach. Immediately, Coach Reese understood Darryl's motives behind his failure to call. Coach intentionally did not dwell on the injury but focused more on showing an interest in Darryl as a young man. Coach knew the injury would heal, but the real repair would come in establishing Darryl's self-confidence beyond sports. That would take time and patience.

Darryl's situation was typical of the kind of problems Reese encountered just getting city players onto the court to play basketball. In fact, Darryl would become the poster athlete for the city player's trials and tribulations that accompany getting from the hardscrabble streets to the sanctuary of the basketball courts.

In addition to Darryl's lack of self-confidence that almost derailed his AAU experience before it began, Coach would have to address other circumstances that revolve around the fact that children often have to make adult decisions out of necessity, whether they are equipped to do so or not.

Sometimes, you wonder how an individual in Darryl's situation keeps the enthusiasm of youth amid all the turmoil that surrounds him. Coach Reese would often pick up Darryl at a cousin's or uncle's home. He recalled going into the apartment of a relative where Darryl said he was staying and feeling very unsure and tense about the surroundings. It was nonstop activity—agitated adult folk coming and going with the frequency of a rush-hour bus stop. Coach's instincts told him that this was not the best environment for a fourteen-year-old to accomplish anything positive.

Coach would pick Darryl up at different addresses. It became commonplace for Reese to drop Darryl off at one address after a Friday night game and pick him up for a Saturday morning game at yet another site a couple of blocks away.

For some city youth, the place called home is often a tenuous arrangement. Moving from location to location happens quickly and for a multitude of reasons, none of which is the child's responsibility. During his six seasons of AAU, Coach Reese had several players from age thirteen to eighteen who dealt with stressful home environments where having electricity, phone service, and heat in the winter was uncertain. Coach would pull his SUV in front of a home to pick up a player and the house would be dark. Unable to reach the player by phone, Coach would hit his horn or knock on the door. After a few minutes, a moving light would appear, perhaps a candle or flashlight, and shortly thereafter the player would spring out the house and hop into the car as if nothing had happened. Privately, Coach would engage the player, asking if everything was okay and if he could be of assistance. The youngster would reply that everything was fine.

This type of brief conversation, with minimal feedback from the player, was the norm. Young athletes, despite going without many ordinary comforts, had deep pride and would not consider themselves poor. Coach recalls that when the players of his 14 & Under team lobbied him to compete in an out-of-town tournament, he told them that in order to find the necessary funds for the trip they would have to help with fundraising. Coach suggested a car wash or donut sale, a typical strategy for AAU grassroots programs to garner cash. Perhaps the most recognized way grassroots inner city programs raise money is simply taking to the street corner, wearing the team jersey, bucket in hand with a friendly smile, and asking for donations from cars stopped at red lights. While Coach saw the value of this fundraising approach for small grassroots programs, he didn't want this for his own players. He wanted his young men to work, on the court, in the classroom, and in life. But just to seek a reaction from his players, he suggested they solicit donations at a busy intersection in town. The players in unison bristled, "We ain't standing on no corner like we poor or something!"

Yet the lack of money was always an issue with most of the players. Clearly the warning from the three wise men about the lack of funds in dealing with city boys was prophetic. Needless to say, this wasn't a problem for leaders like the three wise men who believed that making money was the preeminent goal. Coach Reese had other objectives in mind. During the six years of his AAU stint, probably 75 percent of Reese's players simply would not have been able to participate in AAU basketball without Coach Reese and his assistant Clarence Claiborne reaching deep into their wallets.

Chapter 8: A Honey Bun and Cream Soda

A successful and principled business and community man with a strong commitment to compete, Reese was able to solicit money each and every season to support his program. This included funds to pay for gym time to practice (often through the county or a janitor to open the gym), tournament entry fees, and trips, including expenses for hotels, rental vans, gas, and food. It also eventually included plane fares for out-of-state and cross-country trips. In most grassroots AAU basketball programs, these costs are generally passed onto the parents and guardians of the players. These costs, combined with the bottom-line, profits-driven attitudes of program leaders like the three wise men, clearly make AAU participation a pricey venture and increasingly exclusionary for players with families who don't have discretionary income, like most of Coach Reese's players.

Coach Reese was aware of this scenario going into AAU and had planned accordingly. However, he did not anticipate that his players would not only lack money but also would not communicate with their parents or guardians about money, would not properly prioritize the resources they had, and would not have a proper value system regarding money.

At every turn the young athletes needed help. From the most innocuous situations, such as Coach advising a player to ice a sprained ankle, to which the player responded "we don't have ice at home," to the heartbreaking circumstances where player and family were evicted, money issues were omnipresent for the players.

In the second season of his program, Reese organized weekend out-of-town trips for his 14 & Under team. For some it would be their first overnight, out-of-town trips. The team would leave for, say, a two-night hotel stay in Hampton, Virginia. Coach was somewhat surprised because many of his players needed him to pick them up as parents certainly were not going and perhaps didn't even know their sons were heading out of town. Coach also was stunned to discover that the players had not packed a thing, not a piece of luggage or a carry-on bag. Maybe they had a backpack, but that was the extent of their preparation for the three-day trip. If they brought any money with them, it surely was not enough for meals for three days. On many occasions, Coach Reese and Coach Claiborne would have to run to Wal-Mart to buy everything from socks and underwear to deodorant and toothpaste for players. Nevertheless, Coach Reese saw this as part of the educational process and exposure he was trying to provide the athletes.

Thought processes about money and its value among the players and their families were problematic. After all, the youngsters all had the requisite state-of-the-art attire: baseball caps featuring the various pro teams, color coordinated with costly, cutting-edge sneakers they wore for show only and not competitive play. They also had a second or third pair for the games. And of course, shiny headsets provided music for the head-bopping, shoulder-rolling strut of a true baller.

Some parents who could afford to go on these trips believed that Coach was being "pimped," that the athletes were taking advantage of his generosity. Indeed, from a distance, that observation could have merit. But there was a thin line between families taking advantage of the situation and those truly in need. The athletes in Coach's program were in the second year with him. They had come to rely on Coach for transportation to and from games and practices, for the teaching of the game of basketball, for scheduling of games, and for meals while playing from sunup to sundown. So a certain expectation had become a part of the relationship. The players reasoned they needed only to play, work hard, follow instructions and stay out of trouble and Coach would take care of everything else.

Furthermore, an athlete under Coach Reese was not going to pull a fast one, primarily because Coach believed in and established accountability. Reese expected the same thing from every player, regardless of his talent level. Accountability was demanded on and off the court. If a player thought he was on a gravy train and the AAU experience was about him, he would shortly discover that a young teen is not mature enough to tangle with a coach this savvy. Coach Reese would address attitude problems with players, and even with parents and guardians at home. He called out tardiness off the court and selfishness on the court. And soon the player, acting on his own account, would simply cut himself from the roster. The players who stayed in Coach Reese's program for the duration learned accountability, work ethic, and trust, with basketball sprinkled in for good measure.

Lastly, because Coach Reese was raised on the same DC city streets—albeit thirty-some years earlier than his players— he knew and understood his athletes. He had the trust of his players. He was the one who had been to their homes, had met with the parent, grandparent, or guardian. He is the one who got the late-night call when a home emergency took place and the young athlete was truly frightened.

Whether the athletes acknowledged they were poor or not, they had needs. Often Coach would get calls before school would start in September, and a trio of athletes would ask if he could help with back-to-school supplies and clothing in some cases. And virtually every time, Coach would assist not only with money but with transportation to and from the mall. Whether Reese knew at first that this would become part of his assignment, it did not matter. He was keenly aware the players needed and trusted him. They indeed had financial hardships from time to time, and he felt compelled to help. He was accountable to them after the AAU seasons ended.

Darryl played four seasons for Coach Reese's program, and soon the housing situation for his mother and younger siblings stabilized. Still, other issues surfaced in which it seemed like he wouldn't get a chance to play at all and maximize his athletic talents. Darryl, it seemed, would run up against every roadblock.

After several incidents, including receiving threats from gangs and being chased home numerous times, he considered transferring from Theodore Roosevelt High School in the northwest section of the city. After a friend was killed in a neighborhood beef among rivals, Darryl was suspected as being from the same housing development and brutally targeted. This time, he transferred away from his neighborhood school to Kamit Institute for Magnificent Achievers, (KIMA) a DC Charter school.

Changing schools proved to be a good decision for Darryl as it related to safety, but in other areas it was difficult. Charter schools have different guidelines, requirements, academic rigors, and disciplines than public schools have. Consequently, Darryl struggled with everything from his grades to meeting the proper dress code. Often, Coach Reese, again serving as his player's emergency contact, was called to the school to save Darryl from suspension or in a couple of cases get him back into the classroom. Generally, the transgressions ranged from disrespecting teachers to dress code violations such as not having a tie. Fortunately, Darryl was able to maintain grades well enough to stay eligible to play for the school and Coach Reese's program.

Chapter 8: A Honey Bun and Cream Soda

Along with a sometimes-rocky home environment, a high incidence of street violence, academic challenges, behavior issues in the classroom, and the pressure to make independent adult decisions without the knowledge to do so, there can be other major challenges to getting a player to the basketball court and keeping him there. Often overlooked is the health and diet of young developing children.

Darryl complained repeatedly about tooth pain, and Coach Reese had to work his contacts to get him to a dentist for a nominal charge, which Coach covered. Apparently, Darryl had so many problems with his gums and teeth that the dentist wondered how he was able to eat without pain. Often dental and medical checkups and treatment are secondary priorities for struggling families in the city, and in rural communities for that matter. That is, they are secondary until something happens requiring an emergency room visit at the hospital. Because the lack of insurance precludes preventative visits and checkups, many youngsters just press through the discomfort and pain. However, this can stunt growth and development.

Nutrition and diet is another subject that families in these communities rarely discuss. Unless students are on free lunch programs, a regimen of three meals a day is sometimes a pipe dream. Even when school lunch programs are available, there is plenty of junk food children eat and plenty of nourishing food they discard.

On one frigid wintry morning in March, when Coach Reese arrived to pick up Darryl for a game, he was floored by what he saw. Not only did Darryl rush to the car without a winter coat, wearing just his uniform jersey, but in his hands were a honey bun and cream soda. This grab-n-go, non-nutritious, sugary breakfast was actually an upgrade. Most of the time Darryl and his teammates, though they knew they were possibly about to play three to five games, arrived to a tournament without any food in their stomachs.

Realizing the importance of nutrition, Coach Reese often bought breakfast, lunch, and dinner for the athletes. Yet, due to the hectic and on-the-fly schedule changes at tournaments and in leagues, often the best a coach can do is buy fast food. In those cases, Coach Reese would grumble about how the pickle in a McDonald's burger would be the closest his players would come to a green vegetable in their diets.

Despite all the obstacles, once Darryl finally got on the court he was an exciting player to watch. You could not help but marvel at his coordination, raw athletic gifts, the projections for his body development (should he remain healthy and take proper care of himself), and, of course, his toughness from having played football. This is a real and often understated advantage for some players. Often football guys make the move to basketball and seek contact, play through contact, and shrug off contact throughout a game. They don't become distracted or intimidated and, in fact, appreciate the more physical games. Darryl was this type of player.

Yet Darryl had one flaw that could derail his productivity. He would let referee calls distract him and would contest their calls. He could be playing very well, but a couple of travel violations or a block-charge call against him or a teammate would make him lose focus. Soon, a technical foul for arguing with an official would follow, leading to a benching from Coach Reese. Upon Darryl's re-entry into the game, inconsistent play would be the norm, generally leading to another technical foul, fouling out, or both. It was amazing to watch Darryl—a young man with the perfect personality for a team sport on and off the court, a youngster you instantly liked, especially given his background—self-destruct because of referee's calls.

Coach Reese theorized that Darryl's rough-and-tumble environment, where he pretty much raised himself, led to a distrust of authority, which led to his contentious relationship with referees, the game's main authority figure. Nevertheless, Coach would have discussions with Darryl about team leadership and controlling his emotions and staying focused. He also had me speak with Darryl, as I was with the team at practices and on the bench for games whenever possible, and Darryl knew I was a referee. Darryl would always nod in agreement, flash his hundred-watt smile, and promise to do better. He didn't hold that promise for long, it seemed.

As Darryl matured, his interactions with referees improved. Yet at the same time, better-skilled basketball players with equal and better athleticism passed him by. This in turn led to displays of frustration on the court, which Darryl would blame on the officials. The recipe led to a no-win situation and inconsistent performances from game to game. He would remain in the starting lineup but eventually see his minutes compromised in Coach Reese's program. Yet, he never complained or entertained quitting and remained a good teammate and leader for the other players. He finished what he started as it relates to competing in Coach's program every season.

Darryl started all four spring & summers in the program. After graduating high school he went on to attend Montgomery Community College in Rockville, Maryland. He would get his associate degree, although he did not play basketball. Today he is still living in the city and is gainfully employed, and he closely monitors the athletic development of his younger brother, who plays high school football and basketball. He also stays in contact with Coach Reese.

Playing Time: Tough Truths about AAU Basketball, Youth Sports, Parents, and Athletes

In the world of AAU basketball in the inner city, Darryl's story of overcoming roadblocks is far more the rule than the exception. It is a success story that easily rivals the rages-to-riches tales of supremely talented athletes overcoming their environment en route to becoming an NBA lottery pick. After all, many people will assist the gifted prodigy, but who will support the unnamed marginally talented player to become a productive citizen as he travels the many detours and obstacles of inner city life? In truth, most athletes don't get to college through AAU or competitive travel sports or high school participation.

Darryl's success is underscored by his perseverance. He could have quit many times like others with similar circumstances did, and dwindling playing time in Coach Reese's program truly tested his dedication. So many black male athletes in the 13–17 age bracket, having been repeatedly disappointed by not having the kinds of security we take for granted, are quick to make excuses, point fingers, and give in to the fear of trying something hard. For athletes facing those kinds of obstacles, the mantra becomes, "Why bother, what's the use, why have a vision or a dream?" They find victory in just being comfortable today, even if that means being counterproductive and self destructive. Yet Darryl wanted more and pushed for more. To Coach Reese, Darryl's growth and development made him an NBA lottery pick in life.

Coach Lang Reese and his program and players like Darryl and DeWayne are the true faces of AAU and competitive travel basketball. The story of Coach Reese and his players will be the best-case scenario for perhaps 90 percent or more of all teams. Coach Reese met his corporate mission—most of his players had the opportunity to compete in front of some of the top coaches in college basketball. And certainly they grew as young men as well as basketball players by participating in his program. Still, only two players out of the forty-five players who competed for Coach Reese during his six seasons of AAU played Division I basketball. Three others played D-II, a pair played D-III, and three more played JUCO (junior college) ball. A trio played football in college. All made their varsity high school basketball team. This is an exceptionally high rate of Sports Pyramid success and next-level college athletic achievement, especially for a grassroots program not sponsored by an athletic shoe company (which is what the overwhelming majority of AAU and competitive travel basketball teams are).

All of Coach Reese's ballplayers will tell you without hesitation that playing AAU basketball was the highlight of their athletic careers. For many it offered their first out-of-town experience, first hotel stay, and first plane ride. They will tell you how going to a national travel basketball tournament and representing Washington, DC, in competition against other cities and players with big-time reputations was a rush that will never be duplicated. Triple that pleasure if and when they won! The bottom line: all would say they will never forget their experience.

Understandably, most parents hoped for a college scholarship when they entered the AAU scene. But there is no downside when young men like the alumni of Coach Reese's program reflect so positively about their AAU experience. If there is a negative, it is only the unfulfilled and unrealistic dreams of scholarship-hunting parents.

Two Worlds of AAU & Competitive Travel Basketball

It seems we constantly hear two sides of the AAU basketball story. First is the story of the hotshot stars—the "next Michael" or the "next Lebron" playing on shoe-sponsored teams that win "showcase" events or AAU national tournaments—who get tagged as top-5, top-10, or top-25 recruits in the country, then sign essentially one-and-done deals with big-time college teams like Duke, Kentucky, Louisville, or Syracuse, on their way to the NBA lottery draft.

Often parallel with these talented athletes are headline reports of the slimy underbelly of backroom money deals by unsavory AAU coaches to entice, recruit, steal, and pay players to change teams and high schools in order to deliver them, by any means necessary, to the highest bidding college program.

Let's be perfectly clear. These scenarios happen mostly among the elite 5-star recruits within the spring and summer youth basketball culture. These athletes, singlehandedly can lift a college hoops program into the Final Four picture with their signature on a letter-of-intent. Consequently, the recruiting process and competition for them often becomes a high stakes, intense and nasty affair. It is why I have issue with the term "grassroots" used by the athletic shoe companies. It is clearly more about big business. Furthermore, and similar to making an NBA roster or even getting an athletic scholarship it is about a very small percentage of the athletes that compete in spring and summer hoops.

The overwhelming majority of players, indeed, fall into the second world of AAU and competitive travel basketball. They compete in programs like Coach Reese and the Blackhawks. They are players trying to navigate the Sports Pyramid, improve their game and get on the scholarship radar. And while some athletes catch the eye of a college coach and receive next level opportunities the majority will not as the volume of players, obviously, greatly exceeds the scholarships available per season. (The scholarship numbers don't increase because of competing in AAU and competitive travel basketball just the opportunity to be seen by coaches).

Bottom line: AAU and competitive travel basketball is a consumer purchase. It has different levels, features and benefits presenting varied choices similar to selecting fast food versus a 4-star restaurant or a compact car versus a SUV. Their mission is not to be confused with philanthropy, and concern for young athletes. It is a profit driven business primarily making money by selling the opportunity to play basketball games to young athletes and scholarship dreams to parents. And those that conduct business under the AAU and competitive travel basketball umbrella do their work well. The mostly three day tournaments are very spirited, competitive and fun for the athletes, and generally well organized. It keeps the players engaged and a chance to improve their individual skills. The event is truly a games intensive, hoops weekend party. And if this were the primary advertisement used to drive the events all would be fine.

But it is not.

The promise of scholarship, exposure, potential and productivity to climb the Sports Pyramid fills the air at these tournaments. This is apparent by the time and money given, intensity and anxiety on display by parents and adults. And it is obvious in the black sports community's belief that basketball conquers all.

The overall picture lacks balance.

Restraint, evaluation, knowledge and an assessment of your goals need to be made before leaping into the fray of AAU and competitive travel basketball.

Chapter 9: Drinking the Kool-Aid of Early Athletic Success

There has been a long-raging debate about the proper age for young players to compete in sports and events such as contrived national tournaments.

The issue shouldn't be as contentious as it is, particularly for athletes under ten years old. Youth sports for this group should stress having fun and learning sportsmanship, the fundamentals of the sport, and the best ways for players to interact with their teammates. This sounds so simple and basic. After all, you would not teach your child to cut meat with a spoon, so why would you allow your child to play baseball with a glove on the wrong hand or shoot a two-hand set shot in basketball? These examples illustrate the physical and mental fundamentals of sports that coaches need to teach along with techniques and mechanics to play the sport correctly.

All too soon, however, the priority shifts from fun and fundamentals to a win-at-all-cost mindset. The catchphrase becomes "We must win," whether it's a CYO tournament or Pee Wee football championship or 10-&-Under county recreation league. Winning trumps learning, intensity bypasses patience, emotion overruns sportsmanship. And it is the adult leaders who push this mindset, not the young athletes out to learn and enjoy the game.

So to feed this competitive beast within, coaches and other leaders start pursuing what they think are creative strategies to win. But in reality, their approach is very unimaginative and limited in scope as coaching staffs have only one or two days of one-hour practice before the weekend games. The young players on their teams have limited skills, and the priority should be on developing those skills, but, alas, this goal has been abandoned in pursuit of winning.

Chapter 9: Drinking the Kool-Aid of Early Athletic Success

With these limitations in mind, coaching staffs decide that winning must be handled solely by their teams' best athletes. This generally entails structuring a winning game plan around the biggest, quickest, fastest, most physically developed, or smartest in terms of understanding the game. Plays are designed to get these players the ball as much as possible. The other athletes with marginal skills do not learn (during games), which is why they are in the youth league in the first place. Instead, they are asked to do only one or two tasks, such as staying out of the way and passing the ball to the best players.

The parents of overlooked players leave games happy when their teams are winning because at least their child is getting playing time. In fact, even though the game plan clearly has the best players monopolizing the ball, they comply, acknowledging the difference in size and speed between players on the team, including their child, and the obvious athletic gifts of the star. It doesn't necessarily bother them that, for instance, their child only was given one at bat and was hidden in the outfield, never got a kick on goal in the soccer game, or never attempted a shot in the basketball game. If their athlete is happy leaving the gym after a game, the parent rationalizes that the win is a good thing even though game fundamentals and skill development were neglected. One thing about youngsters: win or lose, ten minutes after a game, get them a soda from the concession stand and they are happy again. Interestingly, even in losing situations, parents make excuses that the other team's best players were older or played the entire game, which of course they say was against league rules. Their primary focus is on why the game was lost and not the fact that the athletic skills of their child were never on display.

The parents of the stars, however, have a totally different post-win experience. They receive hand slaps and hearty pats on the back for the accomplishments of their athletic prodigy. Compliments flow freely about the talents of the young athlete. Predictions are made as to where the player is headed in his athletic career and how this dominant performance that just took place will remain the norm in the future. The accolades are indeed sincerely given, particularly when the young star just led his 11 & U team to that highly coveted church-league semi-final win. Adults caught up in the sugar rush of the win have glazed over what should be the priority: sports development and sportsmanship. Their misplaced emotion is a spontaneous and reflexive instinct to win that organized competition nearly always induces.

For these proud parents, the enthusiasm brought on by the victory and the praise from other adults, combined with the success of their larger, bigger, and faster star mixes together to form the sweetest tasting athletic smoothie a parent can drink. The early athletic success produces an irresistible concoction of athletic dreams that will surely lead to Sports Pyramid next-level accomplishment, with all the benefits and features that follow.

Yet lost in the euphoria of wins and dominant performances is the truth about how those things came about. Instead of fundamentals and pure basketball skills determining success, the deciding factors were size and strength, speed and quickness, and instincts. But nobody really seems to care as parents and even coaches have already begun to taste the intoxicating drink of sports celebrity.

The "Meal Ticket"

The parents of stars become lulled into believing that this type of status and early success is sustainable. They believe that all the attention they and their athlete are receiving from recruiters of middle-school teams or private schools and from recognized AAU and competitive travel teams, are merited and well founded. Successful games spawn the pursuit of more successful games, as the star's stellar athletic performances, team wins, and the praise of adult peers all become sources of incomparable ego gratification.

Suddenly, it becomes the parents who can't get enough of the athletic success of their child. They become so infatuated with the trappings of success and their child's future prominence that they liberally and seriously refer to their budding star as their "meal ticket." The term extends across all youth sports, geographies, and races. It is used by suburban white parents watching their eleven-year-old star pitcher toss no-hitters on immaculate tree-lined open fields to city-dwelling black parents engrossed as their ten-year-old scores basket after basket in poorly lit, cramped recreation centers. They believe the dreams are supposedly becoming reality. Future success requires only for their star to continue playing games.

Here Come the Dream Sellers

This short-sighted prediction established by uninformed parents becomes a dinner bell for those in the business of selling dreams to athletic families. These individuals are masters of understanding the psychology of parents. They know how to market and promote their agenda. If it is games that parents think they need, games are what the business will provide.

Early athletic success generates a thirst for parents to seek new sports lands to conquer. All of a sudden, parents are no longer content with the church league or the county recreational league championships. They decide it is time for state championships and beyond that level, the national AAU and Pop Warner championships that are the stuff of myth.

Anxiously waiting to capitalize on this feeding frenzy are the well-oiled dream-selling businesses. They pounce with well-organized tournaments marketed so slickly that the consumer experience is the sports equivalent of mall shopping on Black Friday after Thanksgiving. Parents feel obligated to participate.

Ultimately these dream-selling businesses, promote winning above the teaching of fundamentals. In fact, they take the winning-above-all-else concept to another level, requiring parents to make serious sacrifices to participate in tournaments, rescheduling or canceling family vacations and taking long-distance trips with costly hotel stays. This often requires allocating resources that strain household budgets. In those cases, parents double down on their investments, becoming even more consumed with winning and the success of their prodigy.

Playing games is so embedded in the youth sports culture that parents believe that they are doing a disservice toward their child or are derelict in their duties as parents if he or she does not participate in AAU and other competitive travel sports. It is the sports equivalent of making that supposedly mandatory family trip to Disney World.

The claim that playing games is the most important development step in reaching that next level is the greatest fallacy today in youth sports. This myth is artificially promoted and slickly advertised by the dream selling-businesses, and now it is generally accepted.

Instead of feeling guilty and pressured to participate, parents need to understand that game playing is just one supplement among many to next-level success in youth sports. Game playing, by analogy, is like opening the windows in a hot and humid house, while practice and repetition is like using the air conditioner, which is more effective, efficient, and rewarding. Unfortunately for most parents in youth sports today, things are reversed in this analogy. Thanks to the dream-selling marketers, games have come to represent that trusty air conditioner.

Sports Winds Change Direction

At a certain point, parents become completely caught in the web of youth sports. They have seen their athlete take over the competition at an early age. What started as an opportunity for him to learn and have fun has given way to a "meal ticket" optimism with visions of next-level sports star status, creating in parents an appetite for more games on bigger and brighter stages to feed their outsized egos. In all the euphoria of early athletic success, the commitment to fundamentals and skill building, to solitary practice and repetitions, is lost.

Then, quietly and subtly the wind begins blowing from a different direction. As the prodigy moves up in age to another bracket, no longer is the young athlete the fastest or biggest or strongest on the field or court. Suddenly, he is merely "one of the better athletes" and not "the best athlete" in the contest. Unexpectedly, the customary string of stellar performances is sprinkled with a clunker or two, leaving the athlete and parent perplexed and somewhat frustrated.

All of the sudden, fundamental flaws that were previously masked by size and strength, quickness and speed are exposed. It becomes clear that a skill set is in need of improvement if not total reconstruction all together.

The young athlete continues to shine periodically but fails to stand out in games as he did earlier. Next-level recruiters at the middle schools or travel and club teams honor their offers and bring the player into their programs, yet it is not the same as before. He no longer athletically towers above the competition and clearly is no longer the center of attention. Now, instead of going to a next-level team that was going to build around the athlete, he is just one of the players why it should be a winning program in the future.

Even the relationships and dynamics at home have changed. The athlete is still the family pride and joy and certainly the center of attention, but fewer dominant performances of late have led to more scrutiny. Parents ask questions about the player's time management and whereabouts. Have there been fewer outstanding performances due to watching too much TV, playing too many video games, using cell phones and social media too much? Rides from the games and dinner table discussions become more contentious and frustrating. Anxiety rises as the "meal ticket" appears to have hit an unexplainable slump.

The parents lay initial blame on the team and coach, even though this same team and coach helped the player shine in the first place. It must be a case of poor coaching, or the structure of this team is different. Or maybe, according to the family rationale, the opposition is focusing entirely on their athlete and the other teammates now aren't good enough to take the pressure away from their child. In time, the parents will contemplate a change of teams (starting that peripatetic journey of endless transfers). Nevertheless, as the athlete's performances become less and less impressive, more and more inconsistent, insecurity begins to creep into the family sports fabric.

Apparently, the parents can't see or refuse to see what others clearly notice: the athlete is no longer the physically powerful man-child of earlier times. He's now competing against athletes the same size and is struggling mightily due mostly to a lack of fundamentals. The parents, and to a lesser degree the athlete, once intoxicated with early child sports success and once possessing an inflated opinion of themselves, are now left with false pride and a wounded ego, holding on to past athletic success as proof that things will surely improve again.

Unfortunately for some families, this entire sports drama takes place before the athlete even enrolls in high school.

Chapter 10: Making the Right Moves in a Playing Time Predicament

In many youth sports cases there comes a point of significant discord and contention for young players. It happens when expectations and personal goals collide with diminishing playing time and other harsh realities. Parents at this stage usually begin an exhaustive search for reasons and answers as to how to avert the predicament.

Indeed, it can be a very perplexing and tumultuous time as parent and young athlete find that the coach and his staff don't have the same assessment of the athlete's skills and talents. In all the confusion, frustration, and pain, parents attempt to fight back in ways that are counterproductive. They often cry out to all within earshot with theories of sabotage, conspiracies, favoritism, and other nefarious schemes at work behind the scenes. However, in most cases, perhaps as high as nine out of ten instances, none of the above theories are valid. It's simply a story of better players taking the athlete's playing time.

At all levels coaches passionately want to win. It serves them no purpose to have their best players on the bench. But for parents with high expectations of athletic success for their youngster, this axiom becomes null and void in their minds. They replace respect for the coach with contempt and imagine he is out to harm their child. Brian McCarty, head coach of Sherwood High School Girls Volleyball and three-time 4A Maryland State Champions says, "Some parents really do think coaches are staying up nights figuring out ways to get their son or daughter to quit the team!"

The moment of crisis leads to questions that parents need to answer for themselves before embarking on a campaign to discredit the coach. This campaign almost always centers on the lack of playing time their child is receiving. Yet, why is there no talk of reprehensible and devious plots to "get" the star players or other starters? Why is their athlete seemingly the only one being targeted? Why can't the answer simply be that the players in front of him or her are more talented? Or that the problem is the athlete's poor work habits, lack of commitment, or bad attitude? And then there's that elephant in the room: the athlete cannot or will not comprehend or process and execute the playbook, i.e., run a play.

Instead of promoting scandal and defeatist excuses, parents need to make a beeline to meet with the coach to share their concerns in a civil manner. Yet parents don't pursue that option at first, preferring only to attend games. Consequently their bewilderment continues to grow as to why their athlete is not playing ahead of other team members. More post-game discussions with their child—instead of with the coach—lead to even more confusion, which is when the rumors and gossip start. After awhile, things can become so toxic that the parent actually prefers the team to lose as if to show that the coach's poor decision to bench their child is the primary reason.

This scenario is so counterproductive. And while parents can find a sympathetic ear in another parent supposedly experiencing the same issues, most objective observers close to the situation can hear in the parents' rants and hearsay their desperation and lack of knowledge for the sport. In truth, it's obvious that the parents are a large part of the problem. Their actions reflect their ego-driven personal agendas, in which their athlete stands as nothing more than a stage prop.

The Unproductive Parent-Coach Meeting
Some concerned or frustrated parents eventually do choose to speak to the coach, only they decide to do it immediately

after a game, which is far from the optimal time. The sudden inquiry catches the coach off guard, and the unannounced meeting, if the coach agrees to it, will not take place in a private area that offers discretion and solitude. Many a parent will say they have had enough and can't wait any longer and "must get this off my chest," an approach that is a disservice to all involved, especially to the athlete.

After a game, a coach's plate is very full with addressing his players on post-game analysis, collecting uniforms, clearing out the gym, handling media requests, etc. His emotions as well as the parents and fans are high, especially if it has been a close game. Russell Davis, former coach of Academy of the Holy Cross girls' basketball team, which under his leadership won the DC City Title in 2007, says that the worse time to discuss any basketball issue with parents is immediately after a game. "Emotions are running high for everyone," he explains. "It is not the best time for analysis. Wait for things to settle down so that a discussion can be had with a better perspective."

Requesting a meeting before practice is also not wise, since that is always a hectic time during which coaches try to prepare the players in a timely fashion to take the field or floor. The conversation is a delicate topic, and you want to have the discussion as free as possible from distractions and interruptions.

The biggest mistake that parents make in this meeting is bringing up the names of other players and assuming the coach will discuss other players with you. Most coaches will interrupt parents in mid-sentence and inform them that the topic is their athlete and their athlete only. This is obviously frustrating to parents as they want to connect the lack of playing time of their athlete with the extra minutes handed to whom they believe are less-talented players. Nevertheless, the meeting is not a scouting session on the talents of the other players.

The team roster is intact and the meeting is not a debate. Nor is the meeting a court proceeding with the coach on trial as if defending a speeding ticket.

Every season the frequency of parental conferences seems to increase, as does the intensity of those discussions. They're often followed by a player exodus from the program, mostly fueled by parents' frustrations. Coaches will also say dealing with parents and their overzealous expectations for their athlete is the number one reason they leave the coaching business.

Every season parents head to the coach's office armed with a résumé of their athlete's previous accomplishments, an ill-advised and prideful arrogance that the coach does not have the upper hand, and a competitive, even vengeful, zeal to leave the meeting victorious. Only winning the argument should not be the goal. The meeting should be about reaching clarity on the future of the athlete.

If winning a debate, as opposed to holding a fact-finding discussion is the parents' ultimate goal, then the meeting will be fruitless. The parents have already made up their mind that the coach is wrong and consequently will not enter the meeting with an ear to receive. Furthermore, the coach is an expert in this time-tested exercise. In fact, thirty minutes after one parent leaves the meeting, another parent may be waiting in the hallway. And lastly, the coach has the trump card: he is at practice every day with the athletes, and parents are not. Therefore, when the coach begins to speak about practice, which he will inevitably do—you can count on it— parents have lost all leverage. And the coach is right to do so. He is obligated to speak more about practice, as this is where he spends the majority of his time with the athletes.

The Productive Parent-Coach Meeting
The first priority in having a productive meeting with a coach is handling the meeting request properly. Calling the

coach to set up an appointment is always best. It is also a good idea to request a meeting after, not before, practice.

The second priority is to understand the positive dynamics of meeting with the coach. Parents and coach must prioritize the purpose of the meeting, which should be a constructive conversation about the athlete and no one else. The purpose of the conversation should be to come to an understanding of the athlete's role on the team now and going forward. The coach will offer ideas on what your athlete must do to improve.

Sure there will be frustration and confusion regarding the lack of playing time for the athlete, but the discussion with the coach should not be about empire building, ultimatums, and demands. Check that wounded pride, that urge to live vicariously through the athlete and, most important, leave the ego at the door.

Coaches are advocates, and most are also gifted communicators. Meet with him to understand the perspective he is sharing. If parents are sincere about their concern for their child and are not driven by pride, then an understanding or at least a compromise can be found. It may end up a matter of agreeing to disagree. This, too, is okay and can lead to well-thought-out family decisions.

All Revealed at Practice

When I speak with parents concerned about the lack of playing time and ask them if they watched one of their child's practices, the answer is usually no. Observing practice and meeting with coaches should go hand in hand in effectively advocating for an athlete.

The truth will be found at practice. A good coach is a teacher first, so the practice field or court becomes his classroom. It is the ultimate key to finding out what is taking place as it relates to the athlete's progress or lack thereof. Parents place too much emphasis on games. If practice is the coach's classroom, then games are tests or exams. The athlete's amount of playing time is the grade for the exam and is based on how well he or she prepared in the classroom. Practice is where development takes place.

The logic of sports competition dictates no other possible outcome. It actually breaks down to simple math. Teams at the high school level play football games on Friday or Saturday; basketball and volleyball teams play twice a week, generally Tuesdays and Fridays. The relationship between practice time and games played is a 3:1 or 4:1 ratio; any one practice is always longer than any game. Therefore, the true measure of an athlete's status on a team and the best vehicle for a coach to determine his roster and playing rotation is through practice.

Of course, there are inherent problems for parents in attending practice, such as the logistics of making a 3:30 p.m. afterschool session, but if they are addressing the athletic participation and future career of their child, shouldn't it become a priority? If the school principal requested a meeting with parents regarding a classroom discipline matter, surely it would get their attention and they would make the necessary arrangements to attend. The coach and practice should be viewed in this manner.

Working with the Coach on the Practice Issue

Even while acknowledging the value of attending practice, there still is a major potential obstacle, which is the objection of the coach. Most coaches do not want anybody at their practices, including parents, teachers, and administrators. In this regard coaches are no different than anybody else in a work environment; they do not want to be micromanaged. After all, they know parents are already second-guessing them in great detail at every game. It should be noted that this philosophy has been quickly changing since the spring of 2013, when video footage revealed Rutgers University basketball coach Mike Rice physically and verbally abusing players. In the aftermath, many school administrators, while not demanding, prefer coaches to have open practices.

Coaches are very territorial. They bring great pride and passion for the thankless job of coaching a sport. They have deep affection for their sport and the positive impact the sport can make in enhancing the lives of young athletes. At the scholastic level, the multitude of hats that coaches must wear far outweighs the modest stipend they receive for their time and services. Often the total hours a coach puts in during the season far exceeds that of his full-time employment. Today, coaches wrestle with just finding the necessary time in the day to be prepared for all the duties they must encounter. In addition to coach, they often assume the role of teacher, guidance counselor, probation officer, marriage counselor, tutor, equipment manager, taxi driver, truant officer, medical intern, trainer, recruiter, fundraiser, and salesman just to get the athletes to field a team and keep it intact during a season.

Consequently coaches deeply appreciate and value the two-hour-plus practice sessions with their athletes. It is where bonds and relationships are formed with their players. It is the sanctuary and place where they have peace and total control. This is why many coaches prefer to have closed practices.

So when parents want to attend practice, coaches instantly see this as an infringement upon their space the same way we would view a smoker in a non-smoking area, a sick patient sitting too close in a doctor's waiting room, or a driver riding our rear bumper on the highway.

Furthermore, in the controlled environment the coach calls practice, he sees any deviation to the normal practice routine as a distraction. Having parents at practice is considered a huge distraction for the athlete and his teammates. The players know why the parent is there, and coaches worry about their focus and attention to details.

Another concern for some coaches is their style of coaching. Coaches use different techniques to get the best effort and results out of their players. It is the coach's job to find the right tools to motivate and have players reach a high level of athletic attainment. Some coaches get after their players for poor motivation, focus, and attention to detail through yelling and screaming. Often it's laced with profanity, which may or may not be unintentional. They wonder if a parent can handle it, especially when that approach is directed at their athlete.

Coaches worry if the parent can understand the dynamics of the player-coach relationship that they forge at practice. They also wonder in the back of their mind if there is any real value to the parent attending practice. Does the parent really understand the sport well enough to comprehend the mission of practice? Will they really be able to look objectively, or will their vision, as usual, be clouded by the fact that their child is struggling? Perhaps the biggest impediment to the idea of parents at practice is the coach's lack of trust in them. Are parents in the gym to gain clarity about their child, or are they there just to infiltrate and gather information to continue their smear campaign against him and the staff?

Even if you choose to empathize with the coach and understand his bunker mentality, then just what is the appropriate response to a concerned parent making a sincere effort to understand their child's lack of playing time? It is disingenuous for coaches to use poor performance in team practices as the reason for a particular coaching decision, but then not provide parents the opportunity to watch a practice.

Teachers have no problem with scheduling a day for parents to come and sit in on their class. In fact, many teachers endorse and solicit parent participation to help a student who is struggling in the classroom. For parents who are distressed about the lack of playing time for their child, this same type of opportunity should be available.

While many coaches normally consider parents at practice an awkward imposition, they will gladly open practice on certain occasions. Coaches are gracious hosts, for example, when the local media come a-calling for a feature story on the team, school, staff or player, or when college coaches arrive recruiting players for scholarship opportunities. (Can any distraction be larger than having a famous D-I coach on a recruiting visit to practice?)

As a former coach of AAU and competitive travel basketball, and high school basketball, I see the benefits of concerned parents attending practice. I am relieved if parents are caring enough to attend practice because perhaps they can become allies in their child's athletic development. Hopefully parents will begin to see in action the things the coaches are emphasizing to their players and sharing with the parents.

When parents attend practices that I am coaching, I know they see a confident coach with secure knowledge that I am a student of the game, an excellent communicator, and someone who is passionate about the impact of sports and determined to mentor and mold young athletes to be better young men and women through sports. I know the young athletes will learn, and if the parents are sincere and solutions oriented, they will learn too. Perhaps they may learn that this is not the program for them. That is fine.

Parents and their children, however, must understand that they are accountable, too. There are standards and protocols they also must follow. First and foremost, they are expected to follow through on commitments. This is not a pilot program for a player's TV series. This is a team sport, not a collection of players to support a personal agenda. The coach is the captain of the ship. This is not a debate. There are standards that are to be met beyond the court or playing field, which include deportment in the classroom, on the campus, and within the team. Once this overarching goal is established from day one of the season, practice should only become a constant reminder and enforcement of this goal.

The relationship between a coach and parents of an athlete lacking playing time does not necessarily have to be confrontational. It can initiate a process toward forging a successful bond.

Transferring

Although transferring used to be frowned upon, today it is a much more accepted practice and often the result of families and athletes seeking a way out of a perceived youth sports predicament. At all levels, parents in team sports are making the transfer decision at the drop of a hat. There are many contributing factors: too much money invested, too many options, too much parental ego, and too many large rewards as the athlete successfully climbs the Sports Pyramid. Transferring has become as commonplace in scholastic sports as wind sprints at practice. Meanwhile, patience, loyalty, respect for authority, personal integrity and accountability, perseverance, and sacrifice have been shifted to the backburner to simmer.

When school administrators at all levels of high school sports, from city to county to state, convene for their annual post-season meetings, it seems the hot topic is always about the high transfer rate of student-athletes. During several seasons, as school teams prepared for the DC city championships in football and basketball, the sports pages blared with embarrassing reports about ineligible players at one of the schools competing in the playoffs. On several occasions teams have had to forfeit their spots in the playoffs or even the championship due to questions about player transfers. (The fact that these transgressions just happen to be disclosed at the completion of a long three-month season leads one to wonder about the altruistic motives of some program leaders. Amazing that this information mysteriously lies dormant all season, then shows up just before the playoffs.)

Before exploring what's wrong about transferring, it is worth pointing out that families can make the decision to transfer for purely valid reasons. Across the athletic spectrum, reasons and rationale differ. It can be as innocent as the need to relocate the family to another community. Or, the athlete has special academic needs, and his local school can't provide the tutoring required for him. Often many single mothers move their child because they are concerned for his safety within the school and certainly in the surrounding neighborhood.

In other instances, the local high school does not offer a sport, or the program is limited regarding competition level, coaching, facilities, and exposure to college. Some small schools have administrations that do not understand the value of sports and the required commitment to develop and maintain them. Additionally, there are cases where a rising talent outgrows the athletic program, and he simply must transfer in order to maximize his athletic potential.

Chapter 10: Making the Right Moves in a Playing Time Predicament

Often tough circumstances force a family to make the difficult decision to transfer. A coach who recruited a child may leave and move to another program. Financial and tuition commitments may not be honored as new administrations take over at private schools. Schools may close due to financial problems, changing city demographics, and declining enrollments.

Nonetheless, in spite of all these valid reasons, some within the sports field say that the transferring of student-athletes is at an all-time high, which suggests that there is a serious underlying problem. And while most people think the frequency of transferring primarily stems from the lack of playing time and the desperation of parents and athlete to find a happy athletic home, it takes two to tango, and many schools have a welcome mat with red carpet and blaring trumpets leading to their gymnasium. The end result is a combustible mix of hired athletic guns moving from school to school, searching for stardom and a featured role within an athletic program that is similarly looking for visibility and wins to enhance its profile.

Whether parents are accosting their coaches, spinning conspiracy theories about them, or making a rash decision for an athlete to transfer, the "playing time predicament" is often what prompts them into action. There are numerous reasons why players aren't getting as much playing time as they'd like, and perhaps just as many solutions to the predicament. Maintaining objectivity and an open mind is critical. The child's development as an athlete and as a person depends on it.

Chapter 11: The Debate about Athletic Commitment

A clear and useful distinction must be made between 1) parents without sports experience and 2) parents that have competitively played the game at the high school level and beyond.

A large segment of the former is often innocent and naïve on what is required for their athlete to succeed. They believe that their athlete can, with the right guidance and allocation of resources, become a next-level player on the Sports Pyramid. They have confidence in the youth sports process to deliver athletic success.

They are committed to their children and the athletic goals they share with them. These parents are eager for their children to succeed, in many cases because they know they probably cannot afford their children's college tuition without that athletic scholarship. Some parents hope for that pipe dream, the lottery long shot of professional sports success and the financial security it would bring to all. Most of these parents are seduced by the Madison Avenue marketers of the dream-selling businesses working at the big-time national level as well as by the smaller and numerous self-promoters, and entrepreneurs who lurk around the periphery of the youth sports culture.

Meanwhile, the second group of parents, the former athletes, shares the same fervent attitude and many of the same ideas and motivations, objectives, and goals as the uninformed parents. But there is that one foundational point of disagreement.

These parents generally understand that no matter how much time and money is spent, no matter how many technological advancements adopted or next-level strategies employed, nothing will assist in reaching those athletic goals unless a young athlete is one-hundred-percent committed to playing that specific sport. They understand from their own participation in sports at a high level (high school and beyond) that you cannot buy personal athletic success. And they are steadfast in their resolve that the heart and commitment of the young athlete is the starting point to reaching athletic goals, regardless of whether the parent wants it for them or not.

Generally, experienced parents of basketball players have no problem with their children participating in mainstream activities such as AAU and competitive travel basketball or summer camps. But participation is never seen as the end game, only as a tool in the athlete's development. In no way is it a replacement for the hard work of solitary practice and repetition.

The 3 Prong System for Athletic Achievement

Parents with competitive sports experience have a very simple, time-tested framework for athletic success. I call it the 3 Prong System for Athletic Achievement, and it includes building the body, developing a skill set, and expanding the mind. Again, all of this must be triggered, first and foremost, by a commitment to the sport. These parents understand that if the commitment is absent, no amount of dream-selling trinkets and marquee events will lead to reaching athletic goals.

The 3 Prong System for Athletic Achievement emphasizes the value of solitary and repetitive practice, which, it seems, has been replaced by the heavily promoted and highly accepted notion that playing AAU and competitive travel games—and more games after that—are the key to athletic success. The three prongs include the following:

1. Working on the body. This entails proper diet, weight training, cardiovascular training, understanding body mechanics and how to treat injuries, and the value of appropriate rest.

2. Skill building. This constitutes learning and enhancing the fundamentals and mechanics of the sport. These make up the foundation of skill building. Fundamentals and mechanics are only improved upon though practice and repetition.

3. Expanding the mind. This is centered on understanding the game and how to compete. The experience of playing games builds confidence and allows an athlete to reap the rewards of the work he puts in. Games place the athlete in new and different sports situations that require learning how to combine mind, body, and skills to compete and excel.

Experienced parents understand that the success of the 3 Prong System for Athletic Achievement is grounded in a prescription of two-thirds practice and one-third participation in games. If a child is not committed to the discipline of mandatory solitary practice and repetition and instead *only* prefers the allure of playing games upon games in glitzy, overhyped tournaments, he eventually will fall short of his athletic goals. Commitment, and obviously talent, is the single most important key to young athletes reaching their goals. However, there isn't consensus over what that commitment entails. Clearly, the definition of commitment has evolved over the years, causing much debate and consternation among families with athletic children.

One theory that has surfaced is that young athletes today simply lack drive and commitment, especially in comparison to older generations of athletes. At the core of this issue is an intergenerational old school vs. new school debate.

The Old School Quintet

Interestingly, most of my high school teammates from the '70s are successful businessmen, family men, and community leaders now with their young athletes. They eagerly analyze whether their own child is committed or not to a chosen sport.

Felix Yeoman, Dane Edley, Charles Snowden, and Gregory Shields played high school basketball (and baseball) with me back in the day. We played for DC Catholic high school powerhouse St. Anthony High School, which was then coached by John Thompson, Basketball Hall of Fame inductee and NCAA basketball champion coach of Georgetown University. His assistant, Robert Grier, would eventually coach us when Thompson left for Georgetown University in 1973.

We, the Old School Quintet ("the Quintet" for short), are made up of five strong, devoted patriarchs with athletic sons and daughters who have participated or are participating in sports, including football, basketball, volleyball, track and swimming. We have strong opinions on youth sports, and we all believe that reaching athletic goals first starts with commitment.

That principle is based on a sports work ethic that required us essentially to play the game year round. We were required to work out and practice at our little bandbox, the poorly ventilated St. Anthony gym, cold in the winter and sweltering in the summer. Today, for young athletes playing the same sport all year long is commonplace, yet when the Quintet did it in the '70s, it was without the pomp and circumstance of AAU, competitive travel teams, and national tournaments. We did not have the access and myriad options available today, especially during the off season. We played because we had commitment and respect and passion for the game of basketball.

Playing Time: Tough Truths about AAU Basketball, Youth Sports, Parents, and Athletes

The debate today revolves around the issue of access and entitlement. We question whether availability and easy access equal commitment. Unfazed by the bells and whistles trumpeted by the dream sellers, marketers, and others, we contend that hype, convenience, easy access, and parental and peer pressure may force young athletes to play, but can't ensure that they are *committed* to play.

This is not to say that we don't acknowledge the improvements and opportunities for athletes today that were in short supply or absent during our playing days. Nevertheless, we watch with a critical eye to make sure that the young athletes in our families put in the corresponding practice and repetitions, to see if they are abiding by the 3 Prong System for Athletic Achievement.

We also watch for signs of complacency. Is there a lack of urgency to get back to work and improve after a bad game? Does the athlete have an overbooked social or school calendar of events? Do they consider their social calendar more important than reaching their athletic goals? These distractions would never have blocked the Quintet from playing the game.

Another area of contention for the Quintet is passion for the game. We believe that commitment requires passion, and if this is absent, athletes will not ascend the Sports Pyramid. As a result, we are vigilant regarding how our sons and daughters spend free time away from the convenience and structure of youth sporting events. Do the young athletes voluntarily perform the extra work to get better at their chosen sport? Do they watch the pros or college games, or go to high school games to watch their peers or seek information, knowledge, and ideas to get better? Do they read the sports pages, surf the Internet for the appropriate blogs, watch

Chapter 11: The Debate about Athletic Commitment

SportsCenter, or read a sports magazine? All are indicators that the athletes either have true passion for their sport or are playing merely out of duty, obligation, or peer pressure. In our day we would eat, drink, and sleep ball 24/7, and nothing else was more important. This passion, we surmise, was instrumental to our success in reaching our athletic goals. And so we watch our sons and daughters attentively to see if they have the same zeal for their sport.

The philosophy I have described here is not unique to the Quintet. Another major group, coaches, believes that the commitment of the young athlete is open to discussion. Coaches, specifically at the high school level, complain often about the lack of commitment among players and how they are so easily distracted and unable to stay the course. They want the lifestyles and careers of the professional athletes they watch on TV but have no clue of the work ethic needed to get there.

Many coaches believe that young athletes have become so conditioned to playing games and having everything structured and organized for them by adults, including practice and workout times with trainers that they don't know how to think or do for themselves regarding their improvement. Young athletes come to think that what has been set up for them (games, tournaments, leagues, workouts) is enough. They rationalize that if it wasn't enough, then the adults would ask them to do more.

Which is precisely the point made by the Quintet: do young athletes today have true passion and commitment, or are they really playing for a multitude of other reasons? Are they really passionate and committed to their sports goals, or are they playing to pacify everyone in their sports circle? If our sons and daughters, or any young athlete, had the passion and commitment we had back in the day, they would not need to be directed, ordered, cajoled, or enticed to improve their games. Their passion and commitment would provide all the motivation and incentive necessary to improve, reach their athletic goals and climb the Sports Pyramid.

The Generation Gap

I am joined at the hip to the other members of the Quintet. Not only are they my former classmates and teammates, they are my brothers of forty-plus years. The bond we forged four decades ago is still diamond strong. Through sports, we have a fellowship that is time-tested and true. Suffice to say, we love each other. We also love sports and understand the unmistakable virtues and lifetime lessons and relationships that are possible through participating in sports.

As a coach for more than a dozen years and a referee for another thirty, I also have a deep relationship with those in the coaching and referee community. Yet, despite those deep bonds and the views we share about the level of youth commitment, I feel prompted to consider the issue from another angle.

I have an open mind about the issue because there is no denying that youth commitment in sports is under attack in a way that was not seen in prior generations.

As the Quintet watch for evidence that our children lack the same focus for sports as we had back in the day, it must be noted that it is not an apples-to-apples comparison. We never had to compete with the numerous distractions faced by young athletes today. During our playing days, there was no cable TV with one hundred-plus channels, the Internet, social media platforms, personal cell phones, laptops, or video games. For us old school ballers, it was a pleasure just to get out of the house and play sports all day, every day. We didn't need modern technology.

The older generation argues that technology can't be a distraction if young athletes are truly committed and passionate. This is true. Yet, there is no denying the power of technology to captivate young athletes. Interestingly, the detractors are the same parents who purchased these tools in the first place for their children to enjoy. Now that these tools are interfering with the athletic goals of youth, they've become a big problem. The parents' failure to acknowledge the impact of technology on the minds and free time of young athletes is a case of generational bullheadedness. Furthermore, if the older generation took a personal inventory of how many of these same modern advancements dominate their own time, perhaps they would have a more empathetic viewpoint.

Other threats to athletic commitment are a sense of entitlement, impatience, and the lack of accountability. The sense of entitlement stems from the excess of options offered in abundance by the plethora of sports dream sellers. There are opportunities to play and improve everywhere. Athletes and parents become confused about what is beneficial and best. Furthermore, the false sense of entitlement created by the multitude of options undermines players' commitment and work ethic. As an illustration, consider the abundance of teams, games, and events that all but ensure that athletes will make a roster. This means they will not have to battle and compete for a roster spot or try out as past generation athletes had to do. As a result, young athletes today become convinced they can play without having the requisite work ethic and commitment.

Parents, meanwhile, unsure of what to choose for their children, window shop as they try different options with a test-the-waters, lukewarm approach. They are already antsy and impatient as the sports dream sellers have buffaloed them into believing that getting on the athletic track to success— the Sports Pyramid—starts for athletes at age five. Thus the parent buy-in (and it is indeed a buy-in in the literal sense) and subsequently that of their athlete is tenuous and in search of quick athletic dividends.

Unrealized results, usually defined by ample playing time, lead to a lack of accountability and commitment. Parents and athletes simply shop another aisle for athletic success. They know the shelves are plentiful with sporting options, and since the player's commitment to the team was shaky to begin with, moving on is easy and options are plentiful.

Lead by Parental Example

How do we fill in the gap that exists between past and current generations? How do older generations with wisdom to impart teach a sports work ethic to young athletes? After all, the younger generations are dealing with all the distractions previously highlighted. Older generations have a tendency to preach to young athletes on topics such as work ethic, and they use their athletic accomplishments from back in the day as their sermon theme. Generally, this approach doesn't resonate with young athletes. It is all too abstract to them. They relate to the conversation with the same head-scratching confusion that we had when our parents or grandparents told us how they "walked eight miles to school in a snowstorm." "Okay, fine, I ride a bus now," young athletes reply, "So what?"

Chapter 11: The Debate about Athletic Commitment

Perhaps a better way for parents, especially those with athletic experience, to teach a work ethic and enhance commitment and passion is to lead by example. After all, those parents have that required firsthand experience. Whether or not they have the ability to teach the fundamentals is not the most important issue. They can find quality personnel to help in that respect. It is the teaching of discipline, focus, sacrifice, and organization that is essential in creating a strong sports work ethic. As a former athlete and now a parent, I consider leading by example an obligation, not a choice, as it relates to supporting an athlete's goals.

Leading by example first requires showing restraint. Instead of being dismissive of the effects of technology, it is important to acknowledge the hypnotic and time-stealing powers of these gadgets to dismantle the pursuit of athletic goals.

We must understand that young athletes are just that—young athletes. As adults we struggle with our discipline all the time, dealing with a variety of "things we will do better" from diet to exercise to household projects. So we need not be so critical if our athletes drop the ball from time to time as they pursue their athletic goals. It's better to give them that extra push, or if necessary the parental ultimatum of "because I told you to!" They should not receive an indictment that they are an uncommitted athlete without athletic goals.

True, it is hard to determine if parents should push or if it is better to wait for the young athlete to act on his or her own internal fortitude and drive. There isn't a concrete answer. It is a matter of parents knowing their child's personality as an athlete, as an individual.

For example, when my daughter Monica agreed to work out early on a Saturday morning for skill building, fundamentals, and repetitions, I knew she was sincere. A committed athlete, she understood that the 7:00 am early hour at the recreation center was the only time slot available for uninterrupted individual practice time.

Nevertheless, there were challenges. On numerous occasions, after a Friday night of cell phone calls, tweeting, cable TV watching, and internet surfing, my early morning command to Monica to get up was greeted with her rolling over on the bed and replying with a blanket pulled over her head, "Leave me alone." I could have applied two schools of thought to this situation: 1) she was not committed to her athletic goals, or 2) she was a young athlete momentarily sidetracked by the time-sapping, technological toys popular with youth today. As an old school parent who played the sport, I decided on the latter and insisted, strong arm style, that she get out of bed ASAP.

After receiving that directive, she would get ready for the workout. Briefly, she would be mad about leaving the comfy confines of her warm bed and sweet sleep for a dose of winter-morning chill. The ten-minute ride to the gym was usually silent and devoid of conversation. I would only smile. At the gym, her preparation would be lethargic and passionless. Recognizing that nothing would be accomplished with her current attitude, I would dole out the obligatory parent/coach threat. As a committed athlete who knew the benefits and rewards of solitary practice and how it had garnered her previous athletic success, she would then respond by changing her outlook and body language. It would lead to a focused and productive ninety-minute session. Upon returning home, I often would joke with Monica, "Don't you feel good, for now your day is yours. Get lost."

Chapter 11: The Debate about Athletic Commitment

Even with her exemplary commitment and passion for the game, this scenario still occasionally transpired throughout her teenager years. It was okay. I understood it. Having to be the "bad guy"—the domineering parent, some may say—was cool with me. It was a temporary role and only one of the many hats of athletic parenthood.

It was more important that I lead by example in teaching and fostering a strong work ethic in Monica. Later in her athletic career, which included playing at the Division-I college level, she knew how to sacrifice and prioritize events and circumstances to find the time to work on her game. She went on to reach and exceed many of her athletic goals.

Chapter 12: Junior Varsity or Varsity?

As high school tryouts approach, whether or not to join the junior varsity (JV) or varsity team is the sports puzzle that sends parents and athletes to the dinner table for a head-scratching, emotional skull session. Regardless of the sport, season, or gender, whether private school or public, city or suburb, the dilemma is virtually universal within scholastic sports. Resolving the JV or varsity debate is crucial.

What level should the athlete shoot for? Should he or she strive to compete on the junior varsity team and receive the lion's share of playing time or on the varsity team but possibly never get any significant minutes in games? The choice goes a lot deeper than just showing up for varsity tryouts and being content with the decision of the coaching staff. In today's youth sports climate of intense competition and lofty dreams, the JV versus varsity question has become a central family decision.

Thirty or forty years ago, the JV/varsity choice did not pose such a dilemma as it does today. Then again, the paths and progression within youth sport were more defined. Patience, respect for protocol, and the willingness to wait your turn were admirable traits. Scholastic coaches were acknowledged as authorities, and their personnel decisions were generally trusted, respected, and honored.

If you didn't make varsity and you played JV, you were not viewed as a sports pariah. Just the opposite. You were still one of a select group to play sports at your high school. You still had status. You were respected as a player with game. Most important, you had next-level potential and your sports dream remained intact. With effort and hard work you could be moved up to varsity at some point during the season. Even if that didn't happen, you were in the program and would surely make varsity the following season.

Then the perception of scholastic sports changed. Pre high school and off-season programs exploded on the youth sports scene and now everyone feels the rush to reach the next level, climb the Sports Pyramid.

The JV versus varsity question is complicated by the existence of the AAU and competitive travel programs that are offered year round. Athletes' participation in these venues matters because in most cases families have paid to play in these programs. Having shelled out the cash, parents feel entitled and believe they now have a say in whether the high school team roster includes their child. It's an aggressive attitude that says, "Because I've doled out the dollars, my athlete is ready to be a star." Expectations are even higher if the athlete was a "star" in AAU or other competitive travel sports.

Deciding whether an athlete plays JV or varsity can cause just as much consternation for a coach as it can for parents and athletes, as was the case of Brian McCarty, the three-time state champion girls volleyball coach at Sherwood High School, in Montgomery County, Maryland, just north of Washington, DC. At the start of the 2012 volleyball season, McCarty's Warriors were two-time undefeated 4A State Champions. The team was led by two-time *Washington Post* Player of the Year Alex Holston, and ten of its fifteen players were returning from the previous year.

Coach McCarty had a tough decision to make. Should he put two talented sophomores on JV or should he have them practice with and against a talented group of upperclassmen led by the multi-talented Holston? Normally McCarty was a proponent of young athletes getting valuable playing time on JV, but he went against his instincts this time and kept the young players on the varsity roster. With a senior and junior laden team, he knew playing opportunities for the rising sophomores would mostly be limited to games that were blowouts and whose outcomes were never in doubt.

What he did not consider was the anxiety and urgency of the sophomores' parents. They thought that since their athletes had starred on club team rosters over the summer, they would receive significant varsity playing time. Shortly into the new season, the parents requested individual meetings with McCarty. The coach patiently tried to educate the parents about the chemistry and limited playing time available for their girls, especially since they were on a defending two-time state championship team with a roster of upperclassmen. He recognized the promise of the young ladies in the future but explained that this season patience and learning were the keys to a successful season for the players. The talented athletes understood this from day one and were content to work hard and practice hard to improve. However, their impatient parents felt differently. They leapfrogged McCarty and sought out a meeting with the Athletic Director. The meeting was fruitless, and nothing changed.

The players stayed in the program, and the team went on to post another undefeated season and win its third straight Maryland 4A state championship.

As illustrated in the Sherwood High example, the "play versus sit" dilemma is a delicate situation, and many factors are involved in the decision making process. It is also a fluid situation, which it seems the uninformed parents didn't comprehend. The coach can move a productive athlete up to varsity later in the season, or conversely, send a player back to JV as a way to improve. The latter, of course, can lead to a loss of confidence or embarrassment (often felt more by the ego tripping parents than by the athlete). Thus, unless there's been an injury and the coach wants a player to gain confidence and get back in shape as part of a rehab plan, most coaches generally will not send varsity players down to JV.

Moving players up or down has other drawbacks and restrictions. Practicing with new teammates or alternating between two teams can be unsettling for the player and the teams. High school federations or leagues usually have various rules on the number of games an athlete can play on both teams.

There are some very important considerations that parents and athletes need to earnestly discuss at the dinner table regarding that pre-tryout decision. Some have less to do with physical talent and more with the mental makeup of the athlete. Objectivity is essential.

The Case for JV

If an athlete is clearly on the varsity/JV borderline, then he will probably be a starter on the JV team. This means that he will be in the game and will receive all the playing time he can handle. His physical talents will be on display. His talents and productivity will mean the difference between winning and losing. As one of the team's better or best players, he will become the focus of the opposition.

He will also have to expand his skill sets and improve his game in areas that probably kept him from varsity in the first place. Perhaps just as important are the ways in which he will focus on character building, growing in maturity, and personal confidence. This aspect of growth can come from playing complete games and being the team leader.

In his newfound role as a top player, the athlete needs to become a vocal team leader. He will have to lead by example in games and practices. If, for example, the athlete is shy by nature and reluctant to exert his personality, he will no longer have the option to fade into the background and skirt leadership and responsibility. Logging major minutes and having star status require stepping out of the shadows, refusing to blend in with other team members, and becoming responsible for the direction of the team. For example, the last shot to win or lose should become the athlete's assignment; no longer can he be content to defer to other teammates.

Through playing time on JV, physical skills are improved and expanded. Personal growth develops as it relates to responsibility, accountability, good decision making, and leadership. These aspects of growth, often deemed insignificant by certain misinformed parents in youth sports, are necessary for moving to the next level. More important, they are essential for the maturation of a person off the court and playing field.

The Case for Varsity

The reason why an athlete on the varsity/JV borderline would try out for varsity, despite the likelihood of not playing in games, generally hinges on the premise that the player will improve through daily practice and competition against older and better varsity players. Determining the validity of this premise first requires understanding the numbers game behind practice, which many parents fail to grasp.

A borderline athlete will probably hold onto the last one or two roster spots if he makes varsity. Most coaches have enough players on their rosters to field a first, second, and perhaps a third team. Initially the athlete will likely be on the second or probably the third team, which begs the question: how much skill development will actually take place at varsity practice?

Sure, the athlete will take part in skill building and conditioning drills, and absolutely he will receive good coaching from the varsity staff, at least periodically. But the team's numbers just won't work in his favor in that he won't scrimmage with or against the better players. For example, on a basketball team with fourteen or more players, the numbers dictate that only ten players can take the floor during a scrimmage. This means that the athlete on the third team will have a lot of idle time watching instead of participating. He will participate only sporadically, receiving a comparable number of playing time minutes as he would in real games.

Gary Lampkins, a former high school head basketball coach at Dunbar High School in Washington, DC, where he won a city championship and sent several inner city players to college on athletic scholarships, faced the varsity/JV decision regarding his rising sophomore son, Javae, at perennial hoops powerhouse Riverdale Baptist High School in Prince George's County. Lampkins decided that for his son, competing daily with the varsity was more beneficial than playing time on JV, and so Javae tried out, and made, the varsity team.

An excellent coach and teacher of fundamentals and a personal trainer to NBA pros such as Nolan Smith and Jeff Green, Lampkins had no reservations about personally training his son. Lampkins put in the necessary work to improve his son's skill set. He had coached and would continue to coach his son in the vaunted DC Assault AAU basketball program. He believed that "iron sharpens iron" and that practicing against the best competition day in and day out would increase his son's physical skills while forcing him to compete. He would learn mental toughness and fearlessness and to never back down from a challenge.

The plan was indeed commendable as it had vision, forethought, structure, and merit. Most important, and in a way that differed from how most parents handle the varsity/ JV issue, Lampkins used a roll-up-the-sleeves approach and got actively involved in the athletic development of his son, as should any talented coach and student of the game.

The only problem was that the Riverdale Baptist Crusaders, annually a top-10 team in the *Washington Post* basketball rankings and excellently coached by Lou Wilson, was like most private schools with good sports reputations in that it had a deep fifteen-man roster of veteran athletes. Javae was unable to get meaningful scrimmage time against the best players. In fact, Lampkins often would pick up his son from school and go to a recreation center to work on skills *before* practice. Lampkins had decided that there was just too much idle time for Javae at practice, and as a result, his skill set and conditioning were regressing rather than progressing. After the season ended, the family decided that Javae would transfer and play at another school.

The End Game

Resolving the varsity/JV dilemma is a big step for an athlete. However, it does not need to be open heart surgery or result in a trip to sports Siberia. Young players should remember that their athletic lives are fluid, and they can keep pursuing their sports dreams. The measures of hard work and determination required to reach those dreams will remain intact.

Chapter 12: Junior Varsity or Varsity?

If you are a parent of a player and there is a significant varsity/JV debate regarding your child, seek a conversation with the coach. Ask for his or her assessment of the situation and for his short- and long-term plans for the athlete. Ask about the actual practice time that will be available. But in the end, the athlete should always try out for varsity. Whether he or she makes it or not is not the issue. Learning to compete and accept a challenge is the important thing. It is the essence of sports.

Chapter 13: The Office of High School Head Coach

Three and four decades ago, the title of high school coach was held in high regard. In the eyes of young athletes, the coach was the most dominant authority figure in the school, often more powerful than the principal.

The coach was a teacher of the sport, and away from the game, a confidant and advisor. He or she was the primary driving force in a player's progression, perhaps to the next level of college play. It was a privilege to play for the high school coach and not just a formality. Parents were advocates for the position of coach and the decisions he or she made and, at a minimum, lent their support by acknowledging that position's authority.

This is not the case today. Now, the high school head coach is the toughest job in all of youth sports.

The reputation of the high school coach and authority of the position has been both reconfigured and marginalized. In most cases this status downgrade hasn't occurred at a particular high school, but it has certainly happened within the larger culture of youth sports.

The decline in appreciation for the high school coach, traditionally one of the more effective teachers of the fundamentals, has ultimately meant fewer opportunities for players to undergo the proper training in their development as athletes and individuals.

A litany of trends and developments in youth sports has led to a growing distrust and disrespect, especially among misinformed and antsy parents, for the office of the high school head coach:

1. Early access and the single-sport focus. Youth today play competitive sports starting at age five and under, which is upwards to ten years before they enter high school. In many cases, their parents have adopted an all-eggs-in-one-basket approach, essentially having them commit to playing only one sport at an early age. As a result of this experience and training, many parents 1) incorrectly believe their child has arrived to high school with all the experience and fundamentals to excel, and 2) have a desperate need for athletic success as they are all-in with this one sport, thus ramping up the pressure on athlete and coach to provide next level success and moving up the Sports Pyramid.

2.   The multi-lane highway of youth sports. There are so many lanes for young athletes to take on the highway of youth sports today, and all of them supposedly lead to a dramatically improved game. Along the way players have continued to increase their exposure to achievement. Examples abound and include tout sheet rankings for players still in elementary school, berths in AAU national tournaments, and verbal scholarship offers to eighth graders by prominent college coaches. Naturally, the parents of these players believe that by the time their children enter high school, they are equivalent to a well oiled NASCAR machine, needing only an oval track and race to excel. Young players may have improved skills but the tradeoff with increased expectations and impatience by parents is problematic.

3.   The confusion about athletic success. Parents rightfully celebrate the sports accomplishments of their children, but many also let that early success get to their heads. In addition, they fail to differentiate between different levels of achievement in youth sports and what that means for a player's chances in making the high school roster. Today, there are so many choices and opportunities to play in games and have success—win and accumulate impressive statistics— but it doesn't guarantee a starting assignment on the high school team. The games are not apples-to-apples comparisons. For example, a player's success in Division II and Division III AAU basketball is different than another's at the more competitive Division I level. Moreover, parents' egos can be further inflated when recruiters at all levels of youth sports such as AAU and competitive travel basketball, neighborhood

& recreation, and private school adult coaches enter the scene, expressing how they "need" your athlete for success. What many parents fail to understand is that the pitch of these recruiters is part of a larger recruiting blitz. Recruiters, beholden to their business model, have to make the requisite number of pitches, or sales calls. Nonetheless, their flattering attention can give parents a misguided and inflated view of a child's athletic skills by the time he or she enters high school.

4. Anticipated return on investment. Parents believe their significant investment of time, effort, and money in their child's sports career that began at age five will reap high rewards, such as a starting position and star status on the high school team. After all the sacrifices, parents believe that a stellar high school athletic experience is a given and part of the natural progression toward a successful career.

5. Increased scrutiny of coaches. In recent years, the conduct of all school staff, including coaches, has fallen under critical review. As a result, coaches have had to reassess their techniques and styles and how they reprimand and discipline players. Their corrective measures and methods are often challenged by parents and athletes, even matters that were once considered standard coaching decisions, such as selection of starting assignments and distribution of playing time. This amounts to a fishbowl effect that disrupts the entire relationship between coaches and players.

6. Lenient transfer rules. In earlier chapters I documented how players today transfer frequently and quickly and how transferring is now viewed as an acceptable and expected rite of passage in today's sports culture. Now that athletes and their families have this perceived bargaining chip of moving at the first hint of discord (over playing time or a similar issue), the high school coach is forced to assemble individual teams each season as opposed to building his program. He can't count on players to stay at the school their entire athletic career.

7. Decisions to Reclassify: In today's climate, if transferring is considered scholastic sports number one problem then its partner in crime is reclassifying. Parents are making decisions for their athlete to repeat a grade in school in order to allow the player to get stronger and better athletically. This parental decision is taking place with athletes in high school, middle school or even elementary school with players in the second grade. In years past this was masked as being for academic reasons. Today, it is accepted as a sound athletic alternative especially as it relates to enhancing scholarship opportunities. However, especially for public school head coaches, this again, poses unique problems regarding team chemistry and continuity. Most states have age limits for high school athletes and players can only play a given sport for four consecutive years, thus when athletes reclassify in high school they are frequently transferring from a public school to a private school. Additionally, some players are forced to leave public school programs where all is well— regarding playing time and productivity—because their age eligibility will expire.

8. The perceived superiority of the AAU or competitive travel team coach over the high school coach. Some parents see the AAU season as more important than the high school campaign. Especially as it relates to getting an athletic scholarship, the prevailing sentiment among players and their parents is that the AAU coach has more access and connections than the high school head coach. This misperception is alive primarily due to sensational stories run by cable networks and blogs about club teams, travel teams, and specifically AAU basketball teams. However, the teams in those stories are mere blips on the youth sports radar. The five-star recruits who are featured generally represent the top one percent of recruitable athletes. The majority of recruited athletes will need assistance from a host of caring adults, including the high school head coach, assistant coaches, the school principal and guidance counselor, AAU staff, parents, and others within the youth sports culture.

Summer Season Squeeze

Perhaps the best illustration of parents valuing AAU hoops over high school is summer league participation.

Parents and players meet with the high school coach with intentions to play both sports with the primary emphasis on competing in AAU first, while playing with the high school summer league team a distant second. Predictably, this is not acceptable with many high school coaches. Ulysses Lee, head coach of Prince George's County MD DuVal high school boys basketball, 2015 Maryland State 4A boys basketball regional champion and 2015 MD State 4A Final Four participant says, "You can't serve two masters." Lee notes that several players (and parents) every season, have come to him in a quandary regarding summer ball versus AAU participation.

However, Lee from a coaching standpoint assesses the situation very easily. To him there is no choice. You will participate in his summer program *first*. Says Lee, "The player and parent want me to make concessions for an AAU coach that didn't have the courtesy to contact me, in the first place, to recruit my player—a coach I do not know. Why should I differ to an AAU program? The kid can play AAU if he wants but he will make my summer workouts and games his first priority. I am building a winning program and the work starts in the off-season. I am not trying to win weekend AAU tournaments with no college coaches in the stands and only bloggers filling their heads with over hyped nonsense."

Meanwhile, the AAU coach especially if a player is a rising talent will simply tell the parent not to worry about the coach, he is the one that is going to get him a scholarship and if necessary can find him another high school. Nevertheless, the majority of grassroots AAU programs understand the summer league conundrum and work with the players.

Yet, here is where things get messy. While some AAU programs scale back their activities the need to maintain continuity, chemistry and remain sharp from a team perspective becomes difficult as July is when D-I coaches evaluate players. Veteran AAU coach Lang Reese asks the question, "How can you prepare to be your best for July, the most important month of the AAU season but reduce preparation during June?"

Ultimately, what happens in this hoops tug-of-war is the player and parent, specifically for the month of June, get into a dizzying maze of often travelling to a combination of two practices and or games at two different gyms on the same day with AAU tournament play sprinkled in on the weekends.

Collectively, these trends have one common denominator: the assumption that when athletes enter high school they no longer need the fundamental teachings and game instruction that the high school head coach traditionally provided. They only require the stage and extensive playing time. Some players, with support from their parents, believe they do not need direction on, or off, the court or field. They do not see the need for discipline, nor do they want to be held accountable in other areas including the classroom. Enjoying the freedom to transfer at any time, they clearly want to remind coaches that there are other options if the athletic gifts they have brought to the program go unrecognized.

Despite the ways in which coaches are under the microscope and the floodlight, not just during a particular sport season but year round, despite the constant second guessing on coaching decisions by everyone from school administrators to parents, despite the time commitment and long hours logged (which when matched with a coach's stipend probably amount to less than the minimum wage), through it all these dedicated men and women remain willing to endure and persevere for the love of the game and the chance to teach young people valuable life lessons through sports.

Chapter 14: The Referee and the Fan in the Stands

The youth sports genie is out the bottle. You can't un-ring the frenetic youth sports bell. The driving force of the youth sports explosion is the ability to play games. And more games, and more games. Young athletes eagerly want to play games under the misconception that they are getting better exclusively by being on the court or field. Parents enjoy the games for the supposed exposure and future rewards and benefits they allegedly will bring their athlete and them. The dream sellers definitely want the games as they clearly recognize the money to be made. The demand side, for all involved is, indeed, trending skyward.

What is overlooked is the supply side of having qualified, certified referees and officials working through professional, business minded associations/boards to service the burgeoning youth leagues, tournaments, and games. There is potentially a significant shortfall of trained and certified referees/officials in some areas of the country, and in certain youth sports such as volleyball, lacrosse and even football and basketball that must be addressed sooner than later.

It is an ominous problem that most in youth sports simply assume will take care of itself and generally never give a second thought. They take for granted referees at a game as a given similar to parking lots at the sports facility or bleachers in the gym.

Flippantly ignoring this critical aspect of youth sports could lead to future disaster. Competent, caring, rules-knowledgeable adult referees are just as vital to the teaching of the game, assisting young athletes in understanding the rules of the game, and ensuring safety and fair play as coaches, parents, and administrators.

Becoming a referee is not for everyone. It is a thankless job. Even when you're right, you take verbal abuse. Sadly, another growing trend that merits immediate concern is the apparent increase nationwide in physical incidents and confrontations between referees and fans/parents or coaches. Fan intimidation, hostility, frustration and pressure are probably the primary reasons more men and women do not consider becoming referees. Thus recruiting and safety concerns are joined together. Meanwhile, the demand for games increases.

As a veteran referee of 30 years officiating youth, scholastic and scholarship sports I can see dark clouds swiftly moving over youth games in particular. In some cases storms are already underway as the shortage of referees, fan/parent/coach confrontations with officials and the glut of games have led to some troubling trends that could become the standard in the future. They include:

1. Too quick promotion of referees. Today, in many regions there is already a lack of competent and trained referees to cover games. Sports officials and associations for all youth and scholastic sports recruit for applicants year round. Yet, supply is clearly not keeping with demand. In neighboring counties outside of Washington, DC, some high school football referee associations are assigning high school football games, even playoff games, to first year officials that have not gained the necessary experience and training required to merit this caliber of contest. This is potentially asking for trouble as a critical or incorrect call(s) can determine the outcome of a game. This scenario is not the optimal solution but with recruiting numbers down and youth games increasing it becomes the necessary course of action to get the games covered. The associations are doing the best they can to recruit capable men and women, but even with high unemployment in some regions; these associations are not flooded with applicants looking for a good part-time job. Among novice referees who do apply, many simply quit because they can't deal with the abuse hurled out at sporting events. They simply decide it is not worth the stress.

2. Poorly planned events out for easy money. Huge profits are available in every area of youth sports, and probably the easiest way to make a buck is to organize a league or a tournament. Sometimes it is as easy as meeting a handful of requirements: an authorization from a governing body such as AAU; access to gyms; an event website (which of course has a fancy name implying a tie-in to a national and/or professional association); a liability waiver form; and a pool of available referees, many of whom don't belong to trusted and certified associations. Meanwhile the event organizers will reach out to their former ball-playing boys who will work the event for cash paid at the end of the day. Done. Let the games begin!

Capitalizing on the feeding frenzy in this way will only inspire ill-conceived copycat models of events that are nothing more than quick money grabs. These hasty, poorly planned events often place referees in unsafe, perhaps menacing situations. This is especially the case in urban communities such as Washington, DC, and Baltimore where basketball is king and the sports citizens have an insatiable, yearlong appetite for hoops.

Over the years, I've refereed youth sporting events, both basketball and football, that I knew the moment I showed up weren't the safest environments for me and my fellow officials. Game personnel and tournament organizers either were late arriving or absent, except for the individuals taking money at the door/gate. Adult event coordinators often look as youthful and frenetic as the players.

These are signs of poor event organization, which leads to fan discontent, a frenzied style of play once the games begin, and annoying questions from coaches about rules and game interpretations. Or, in the case of the losing team, the referees don't field questions but instead suffer through verbal confrontations, technical fouls, and unsportsmanlike conduct. On top of all that, there are no security personnel or police on the premises. When a referee senses this type of hustle-for-a-fast-buck event, he does not want his name associated with it on any level.

3. A desperate need for immediate results. As sport-obsessed parents spend large amounts of money on their athletes, including entry fees to basketball tournaments that can cost teams anywhere from $300 to $975 for a three- to four-day affair, their frustrations and anxiety are high. These parents often expect to see immediate dividends from their investments in their children's athletic futures, yet they are often confused by what these "immediate results" should entail. Eventually, this angst is heaped on the referee (as if the referees forced them to sign up), and verbal incidents lead to their ejection from the gym. This can happen at games played by nine year olds! Veteran officials respond to the fury and foolishness of parents with nothing more than head shaking. On the other hand, these altercations can unnerve aspiring officials and force them to reevaluate their decision to become a referee.

Without a doubt, these scenarios will continue. There is just too much money in the dream-selling youth sports business to turn back now. There will be even more games, leading to more parents reaching deep into their wallets, leading to more anxiety and outward contempt for the easiest target of their misdirected and misguided rage: the referees.

One obvious and easy solution is requiring all league/ tournament/game organizers pay to have uniformed police visible and present at games before a referee association will assign officials to work the event. In some events this is already in place but clearly not enough.

Nevertheless, the conversation regarding safety of the officials and the supply and demand for referees for youth sports must begin immediately. The critical problem must be addressed by youth sports organizations, both locally and nationally, working jointly with official and referee associations and boards.

***

Typically at large AAU and competitive travel basketball tournaments more than one hundred teams will descend on a city for a three-day crash course of hoops. Invariably, a scheduling snafu will occur, and two youth teams that had arrived ready to play a game are now using the free time to horse around. The pre-game layup lines have deteriorated into school recess. Meanwhile, coaches impatiently pace the floor, administrators scurry about with cell phones glued to their ears, and fans and parents become fidgety and perplexed by the delay.

There are no referees present to work the game.

Despite all the verbal abuse referees must take from coaches, parents, and fans, challenging our integrity ("You're cheating!"), our knowledge ("That's a stupid and wrong call!"), our skill set ("You're blind, ref!"), our competence ("The kids are gonna get hurt out there!"), and our physical appearance ("You can't get down the court. You're too old/ slow/fat!"), when referees are not on the court at the appointed time, you do not have a game.

Significantly, at this moment all adults realize how dependent they are on referees. You can play a game without a visible scoreboard and a clock. In fact, many youth leagues don't have these at their gyms and fields and simply rely on referees and administrators to handle time and scorekeeping. You can play games without defined visible game markers such as a three-point line in basketball or an end-zone line in football, again leaving officials to determine those parameters. You can play games in poor facilities. When gymnasium roofs leak water onto a corner of the court, and administrators decide to play anyway, a manager or volunteer will towel wipe the floor every time the players move to the other end of the court. Likewise, overused county football fields can become ankle-deep muddy swamps when it rains, setting the stage for an unrecognizable brand of youth football. If necessary, you can also play a game without spectators. On a couple of occasions, administrators at Dunbar High School in Washington, DC, were so fearful of potential violence from rival schools that only essential personnel and the cheerleaders were allowed into the basketball game. I refereed those games. Spectators were not permitted, and there were more school security personnel and city police patrolling the campus than fans.

There are many provisions and concessions that administrators can make to keep games on schedule, but you can't circumvent the need for trained, impartial referees who know the rules of the game.

Without referees you don't have a game.

At this moment it is easy to see the panic and vulnerability in the eyes of parents, fans, coaches, and players. The anxiety of a possible long delay, or perhaps a cancellation, or worst of all, rescheduling the game for another day disrupts future plans. For the young athletes, this is no big deal—another day, another game. The games always come in rapid fire sequence anyway, and they know that somehow they'll make it to the next one. But for adults, their personal schedules are now thrown in disarray. A rescheduled game means another lie to the supervisor at the office, or the postponement of events involving other children, or at least making frantic calls to other relatives to coordinate arrival and departure times for those siblings. All of a sudden, the absence of the referees you love to hate controls your destiny beyond the event itself and interferes with your daily schedule.

Interestingly, at this moment there is a sense of desperation and urgency among coaches, parents, and fans to simply *find* the referees, not crucify, criticize, or despise them as they usually do. If only for a brief moment, all must come to grips with the fact that no matter how good the team, star athlete, or the highly anticipated matchup, nothing happens without referees in the building. They are always crucial to the youth sports experience, just as coaches, players, trainers, and supportive parents are essential.

Humorously, when referees finally do arrive, there are sighs of relief everywhere. Panic dissipates as parents and coaches exchange banter with the black-n-white stripe shirt officials, and they all observe a brief ceasefire. But it is indeed very brief, because seconds after the jump ball starts the game, the refs, once again, become the object of their ire and selfish motivations.

This scenario is laughable because of its irony. One of the rare occasions when referees are appreciated is the moment they are not present for the start of a game.

But being shown appreciation is not why one becomes a referee. In fact, coaches and referees are motivated by the same things. Referees are passionate about the values of sport and how participation in sports can be life enhancing and build character. Referees see themselves as teachers, role models, and authority figures. They have an unconditional love for the positives of sport.

The primary difference between coaches and referees is that referees do not care about the final score, about winning or losing. Their goal is to ensure that both teams have an equal chance to win within the rules, promote safety and sportsmanship, and set an excellent example of leadership, integrity, and professionalism.

***

The scene included a verbal exchange between a parent and referee that was typical in recreational leagues in and around the youth hoops obsessed city of Washington, DC. I was in attendance to support one of my best friends, Charles Snowden, and his son, a talented rising sophomore also named Charles. I had known Chuck for forty years, since we were classmates and teammates at St. Anthony High School.

Young Charles aptly displayed his versatile skills on the court, while Chuck, a sports-obsessed parent who acknowledges the ways sports can build and teach character and encourage personal growth keenly watched. Unlike other parents in the youth sports world, he is very knowledgeable about how to support his child's athletic dreams—most times, anyway. He is also emotional.

So when the opposing squad jumped on young Charles and his team and took an early lead, Chuck concluded that the referee's bad calls were to blame. He engaged in a brief sparring match with the referee, sprouting the standard nonsense about "calling the game fair." In a recreation gym like this one, with a sparse crowd in attendance, catcalls from the stands resonate with referees on a different level than in a packed gym. They can hear the comments as well as everybody else in attendance. Obnoxious and repeated offenders must be and will be dealt with as nuisances detracting from the game, and if diplomacy can't be achieved, they'll be sent out the gym. In this instance the referee had a brief exchange with Chuck and the game moved on. Since I knew both the referee and Chuck, I said nothing, nor did I feel I needed to. Business would be handled accordingly.

Shortly thereafter, young Charles and his team began to play well. Shots that missed earlier began to fall. The coach made some adjustments. Momentum changed jerseys. At this time, another parent leaned over to Chuck and said, "You getting on the refs made him change his calls and now we're winning." Chuck agreed. After hearing that fallacy I could no longer be silent. I asked him if he really believed his outburst had an effect on the ref and changed the game. "Absolutely!" was his reply.

It was the single dumbest statement I've ever heard regarding the supposed impact that fans in the stands think they have over referees. Furthermore, I could not believe Chuck was saying this to me, aware of my background as an official of three different sports for thirty years. (I told him, right then and there, this conversation was going in my book). But while baseless, his statement also illuminated the spectator relationship to authority in general, as fans will yell at referees and coaches alike. They really believe their frustrated blathering can impact the outcome of games.

Spectators become empowered first and foremost by their strength in numbers. Their collective identity provides cover for their false courage and foolish outbursts.

Fans have four sources of fuel that ignite the flames of their defiance.

1. A sense of superiority. Many fans believe they know everything about the game, from rules to strategy. They know more than the referees and more than the coach. It takes a certain amount of arrogance to publicly berate figures of authority.

2. The power of emotion. For fans, emotion replaces logic and common sense. Their mantra is, "At this moment things are not going my way, and I am unhappy." (For these fans, instead of barking at authority, perhaps a pacifier would be more appropriate.)

3. A lack of respect. There is contempt and lack of respect for referees and coaches and the tough assignment they have, along with a selfish and shortsighted vision of what is taking place within athletic contests.

4. An unrealistic view of the fans' role. As Chuck showed me, some fans are egotistical enough to really and seriously believe their running commentary can change the course of a game. This is so unbelievable to a veteran referee because fans simply don't understand what a referee actually hears during a game, especially one with a packed house of spectators. Individual voices and comments are almost impossible to discern. Crowd noise becomes a persistent din and ignored as, say, elevator or department store music.

Inflated self-worth notwithstanding, the beat goes on as spectators' behavior continues to reach lower depths of boorishness. In one neighboring county just outside

163

Chapter 14: The Referee and the Fan in the Stands

Washington, DC, youth football league administrators required all parents and spectators who were sitting behind the home team bench to move to the stands on the other side of the football field. The parents were moved not solely because they were taunting the referees. They were also constantly yelling instructions at their own athletes that often conflicted with those of the coaching staff. How old were the young players? Ten and under!

It's a subtle change, but perhaps assigning parents their own section will gain ground. Generally, parents and adults are the obnoxious louts at youth and scholastic games. Students normally are more agreeable. If, for example, parents were relegated to a high corner of the stands or bleachers, perhaps the games would flow freely for all those in positions of authority.

The seating arrangements may even make parents happy knowing they can ease their frustrations by whining among their brethren. And just maybe they will gaze at the overall beauty of the scene and even come to realize how enjoyable youth sporting events are when they're not displaying poor sportsmanship. Why, they might even become role models.

Chapter 15: Taking the Last Second Shot: Final Thoughts on Youth Sports

In the spirit of that dazzling moment when the clock is winding down and your favorite basketball team has one chance to win the championship with one last shot, here are some final recommendations on succeeding in youth sports:

1. Understand certain timetables. Most high school athletes will tell you without hesitation that their dream is the next level—college scholarship followed by WNBA for young ladies, the same followed by NFL or NBA for young men. The dream should be pursued by athletes and endorsed by parents and guardians. What's wrong with a goal that includes a maximum work ethic, team and individual goals, discipline, vision, sacrifice, and methodology?

However, realistic timetables must be established.

For example, if you haven't received any contact or interest—letters, phone calls—from a Division I college by the end of your junior season and certainly before your senior campaign then perhaps you should reevaluate your options for a Division I athletic scholarship. Perhaps this is the time to consider or even contact on your own Division II (according to the website www.scholarshipshipstats.com in the 2014 season D-II had 306 men & 307 women sponsored varsity level basketball teams, with most offering some form of scholarship) or NAIA programs (230 men & 229 women teams respectively). Division III, does not give athletic scholarships but financial assistance package (421 men & 442 women teams respectively).

College athletic programs and coaches are constantly assessing their rosters. They recruit from more than just the senior high school class (their next incoming freshman group). They are targeting recruits two and three classes into the future

Chapter 15: Taking the Last Second Shot: Final Thoughts on Youth Sports

(i.e., high school juniors and sophomores, even exceptionally talented freshman). This is not the time to become delusional. Instead, think clearly about your athletic goals. Continue to work hard. Situations change but understand that the odds are getting very long and realistically highly unlikely that you will garner that Division I opportunity.

Furthermore, if you are one of the fortunate few who receive an athletic offer from a college program, don't become overconfident with a false sense of entitlement. I have seen parents with an athletic scholarship offer on the table decide to wait after the athlete's senior season was over for a "bigger" offer from an ESPN-televised Top 6 conference program. It never came. The offers in hand were rescinded, and the athlete ended up at a community college program, never to play at a higher level.

2. **All athletes are not equal.** True, there are intangibles in athletics that go far beyond the physical attributes of size, speed, and strength. But in the recruiting game, athleticism, along with productivity and skill set, is what moves the scholarship needle. The classifications of five-star, four-star, three-star recruit, etc., are the jargon of the industry. College recruiters section off athletes under these categories just as young and aspiring athletes evaluate the merits, advantages, and disadvantages of Division I, II, or III.

The athletes that make the showcase AAU national tournaments and get mentioned on ESPN headlines or have football signing day press conferences covered by ESPNU are indeed talented, gifted, and special players. These athletes, men and women (less football), can play. They are indeed the top one percent of athletes competing at the high school level. They have produced in their chosen sport. They have the drive and discipline, heart and commitment, vision and goals that you have. They also have exceptional physical attributes and skills. Interestingly, young players know about these star athletes. Ask them who has game and they will tell you.

However, parents often fail to understand how gifted the athletes competing for scholarships each season. They don't distinguish between 5-star athletes and their child. In fact, many parents compare statistics to justify why their child is just as worthy of a Division I scholarship as any other player. It is an unrealistic assessment of next level progress to assume that gaudy stats (100-yard games rushing in football or 25-point scoring nights in hoops, for example) will equal Division I scholarship offers. Even athletic success in addition to high school, such as AAU, and other competitive travel sports does not guarantee an athletic scholarship. The proliferation of AAU and competitive travel programs clouds the competition level and distorts statistics. There are so many teams and games offered today that the quality of competition and the gaudy statistics they generate must be called into question.

Consequently, even if you are an athlete competing in the AAU and competitive travel basketball, don't assume that you rank among the elite of your sport, are the next prep phenom, or are entitled to receive a scholarship. Frankly, too many parents and athletes competing in these programs swell with false pride regarding athletic accomplishments. This, in turn, gives way to grandiose dreams of high school starring roles and Division I scholarships from ESPN-televised college hoops programs. It just isn't factual. Off-season participation in games via club, travel, and AAU programs is the biggest explosion in youth sports. Almost an afterthought 30–40 years ago, today it is supposedly a must-do for families with athletic youth. These programs have become so well marketed and woven into the fabric of youth sports that parents actually believe they are of greater importance than high school sports participation to reaching next-level athletic goals and climbing the Sports Pyramid. Today, there are so many programs with too many levels, divisions, and classifications and too many games offering opportunities to play. These are just hard facts of the competitive youth sports landscape. It is not a reason to change your dream or quit playing altogether, but a wake-up call in understanding the work ethic and commitment that are required in getting that athletic scholarship. Set your goals,

Chapter 15: Taking the Last Second Shot: Final Thoughts on Youth Sports

but realize that the situation is fluid. Parents and athletes must make an honest assessment of their next-level skills and talents.

3. Strive to excel in more than just sports (You are that gifted). The quest for athletic achievement is fine. Set your goals. Achieve your dreams. The frustration comes when athletes don't have a comparable "second dream" of accomplishment. The sports quest is so all-consuming that athletes and parents neglect to establish a second dream of future success. Furthermore, especially in the black sports community, having a second dream outside of athletic success is viewed by some parents as counterproductive and a distraction to the prodigy keeping his eyes on the athletic prize. This is wrong. They can coexist. It is not an either-or proposition. In truth, this tunnel vision thinking reflects your low self-esteem and low expectations to believe your child can only concentrate on one goal. Our gifted young men and women are more than capable, more than talented enough to have multiple dreams of accomplishment on and off the courts and playing fields. And they must.

4. Sport is what you do, not who you are. Furthermore, if you are fortunate to draw interest from college athletic programs, understand that these schools always have contingency plans. You are not their only choice. This is where intangibles such as maintaining good grades and having a good character make a difference and will often be the tiebreaker as to who will land that last scholarship. Become a well-rounded, perceptive, and responsible young man or woman, not just an athlete.

5. Prioritize Education too. Probably the most frustrating aspect of AAU and competitive travel basketball is the lack of balance between hoop dreams and education by both parents and athletes. There is an "all in" for basketball sentiment but very little discussion about education or alternate plans if hoop dreams aren't realized. In fact, it seems that education—high school and higher learning—is treated as a mere consolation prize in the whole scenario. Poor grades in high school and failure to get the necessary score on the ACT or SAT exams detour next level success for many athletes. Often it is simply a matter of not making education the priority it should be.

While basketball and getting a scholarship dominate the discussion, there is not enough serious conversation about education and career goals off the court and playing field. Ironically, parents can see the future athletic path clearly, but they are vague and cloudy when trying to envision a future without sport in their lives, much less the life of their athlete. "Get a good job after college" is about the extent of their advice when discussing alternative goals away from athletics. Participation in AAU and competitive travel basketball is not the problem; the high-wire walk of total commitment to a sport, any sport, without a safety net of educational alternatives is the problem facing too many young athletes today.

6.   Respect the Game. Compete hard. Train hard. Educate hard. Parents and young athletes must understand one undeniable truth about participating in sports: you cannot purchase athletic success, commitment, and passion. There are no shortcuts!

Perhaps Muhammad Ali, the self-proclaimed Greatest of All Time, best articulated how talented athletes reach the top of the Sports Pyramid through time-honored principles of dedication, hard work, solitary practice, and repetition when he said,

Champions are made from something
they have deep inside them, a desire, a dream, a vision.

They have to have last-minute stamina,
they have to be a little faster,
they have to have the skill and the will.

But the will must be stronger than the skill.

169

Endorsements

"The professionalization of youth sports, turning play into a big business resting on pubescent shoulders, is one of the most vexing problems in our sports world. For any parent involving their child in this world; for any teacher working with young people who dream of athletic superstardom, and for anyone with aspirations of coaching or refereeing our young, there is no book I would recommend more than Playing Time by Kevin McNutt. This is both a brilliant expose, and a navigation manual for a world that too many people enter blindly. There is true wisdom here because it is born out of decades of experience and hard-earned street level knowledge. There is no way I could recommend this book highly enough. Buy five copies: one for you, and four for those around you. We will all benefit if people take the time to read Kevin McNutt's words, and heed his counsel and concern."

- Dave Zirin; Sports Editor, The Nation Magazine.

"In "Playing Time", Kevin McNutt talks about the things no one else wants to discuss when it comes to dealing with the cold realities associated with the hoop dreams that are shared by millions of young people in America. He could have easily titled the book "Real Talk" because he delivers a strong message that parents and student-athletes everywhere should embrace as they embark on this sometimes rewarding, but also frustrating journey in search of athletic success."

-Troy Mathieu
Former College Bowl Executive and Div. 1 Athletic Director; Current High School Athletic Director

"The unique and bold observations of Kevin McNutt regarding youth sports are sure to enlighten, entertain, and even anger, while providing pause, introspection and contemplation. It is a tantalizing read written with compassion, understanding and a from the heart commitment to educate parents and young athletes."

-Allen E. Chin, Ed.D., CAA
(Ret.) Director of Athletics, DC Public Schools; (Ret.) Executive Director, DCIAA